Insights You Need from
Harvard Business Review

THE YEAR
IN TECH 2023

Insights You Need from Harvard Business Review

Business is changing. Will you adapt or be left behind?

Get up to speed and deepen your understanding of the topics that are shaping your company's future with the **Insights You Need from Harvard Business Review** series. Featuring HBR's smartest thinking on fast-moving issues—blockchain, cybersecurity, AI, and more—each book provides the foundation introduction and practical case studies your organization needs to compete today and collects the best research, interviews, and analysis to get it ready for tomorrow.

You can't afford to ignore how these issues will transform the landscape of business and society. The Insights You Need series will help you grasp these critical ideas—and prepare you and your company for the future.

Books in the series includes:

Agile	*Global Recession*
Artificial Intelligence	*Hybrid Workplace*
Blockchain	*Monopolies and Tech Giants*
Climate Change	
Coronavirus: Leadership and Recovery	*Racial Justice*
	Strategic Analytics
Customer Data and Privacy	*The Year in Tech, 2021*
Cybersecurity	*The Year in Tech, 2022*
Future of Work	*The Year in Tech, 2023*

Insights You Need from
**Harvard
Business
Review**

THE YEAR
IN TECH 2023

Harvard Business Review Press
Boston, Massachusetts

Copyright 2022 Harvard Business School Publishing Corporation
All rights reserved
Printed in the United States of America

10 9 8 7 6 5 4 3 2 1

No part of this publication may be reproduced, stored in or introduced into a retrieval system, or transmitted, in any form, or by any means (electronic, mechanical, photocopying, recording, or otherwise), without the prior permission of the publisher. Requests for permission should be directed to permissions@hbsp .harvard.edu, or mailed to Permissions, Harvard Business School Publishing, 60 Harvard Way, Boston, Massachusetts 02163.

The web addresses referenced in this book were live and correct at the time of the book's publication but may be subject to change.

Library of Congress Cataloging-in-Publication data

Names: Harvard Business Review Press.
Title: The year in tech, 2023.
Other titles: Insights you need from Harvard Business Review.
Description: Boston, Massachusetts : Harvard Business Review Press, [2023] |
    Series: Insights you need from Harvard Business Review | Includes index.
Identifiers: LCCN 2022010831 (print) | LCCN 2022010832 (ebook) |
    ISBN 9781647824525 (paperback) | ISBN 9781647824532 (epub)
Subjects: LCSH: Business—Technological innovations. | Industrial management. |
    Success in business.
Classification: LCC HD45 .Y43 2023 (print) | LCC HD45 (ebook) |
    DDC 658.5/14—dc23/eng/20220610
LC record available at https://lccn.loc.gov/2022010831
LC ebook record available at https://lccn.loc.gov/2022010832

ISBN: 978-1-64782-452-5
eISBN: 978-1-64782-453-2

The paper used in this publication meets the requirements of the American National Standard for Permanence of Paper for Publications and Documents in Libraries and Archives Z39.48-1992

Contents

Introduction

When New Technologies Converge   xi

How to think about ethics when tech evolves faster than we can predict.

by Beena Ammanath

Section 1

New Fundamentals

1. **How Brands Can Enter the Metaverse**   3

   Build a strategy for the next frontier.

   by Janet Balis

2. **How NFTs Create Value**   13

   Understanding this new asset class.

   by Steve Kaczynski and Scott Duke Kominers

3. **Stablecoins and the Future of Money**   27

   Will central banks and the private sector team up?

   by Christian Catalini and Jai Massari

4. **The Future of Contactless Commerce**   41

From "pay by face" to AI shopping assistants.

by Mark Purdy

5. **How to Attract Top Tech Talent**   55

*New ways to recruit and retain in a
competitive market.*

by Jonathan Frick, KC George, and Julie Coffman

Section 2

Fresh Takes on Mature Tech

6. **What Leaders Need to Know About the Cloud**   65

*What's next for your company's most efficient,
innovative, and scalable platform?*

by Bhaskar Ghosh and Karthik Narain

7. **Say Goodbye to Cookies**   75

Demand both personalization and privacy.

by Tim Glomb

8. **Could Ransomware Attacks Ultimately
Benefit Consumers?**   83

*Companies take cybersecurity more seriously
when their own money is on the line.*

by Rahul Telang

Section 3

AI for the Rest of Us

9. **AI Doesn't Have to Be Too Expensive or Complicated** 93

   *Move from a big-data approach to a
   good-data approach.*

   by Andrew Ng

10. **No-Code Platforms Can Bring AI to Small and
    Midsize Businesses** 103

    Soon, anyone will be able to train an algorithm.

    by Jonathon Reilly

11. **How Warehouse Workers Really Feel
    About Automation** 113

    *Employees from around the world share their
    concerns and hopes.*

    by Joe Lui, Raghav Narsalay, Rushda Afzal, Ida Nair Sharma,
    and Dave Light

Section 4

Trust Me

12. **Do Your Digital Design Choices Take Advantage
    of Customers?** 129

    *Misleading consumers into spending more can
    hurt you in the long run.*

    by Michael Luca and Fiona Scott Morton

Contents

13. **How Digital Trust Varies Around the World**   **145**

Attitudes, behaviors, environments, and user experiences differ widely.

by Bhaskar Chakravorti, Ajay Bhalla, and
Ravi Shankar Chaturvedi

About the Contributors   **161**

Index   **167**

Introduction

WHEN NEW TECHNOLOGIES CONVERGE

by Beena Ammanath

The Covid-19 pandemic was a catalyst for change in every industry and aspect of business. Facing new constraints and competitive pressures, organizations enacted plans to thrive in challenging environments. It ushered in a new age of accelerating transformation and disruption that shows no sign of abating.

Now, with the worst of the public health crisis behind us, we can see a new business landscape in full light. Technology transformations are happening everywhere in unanticipated ways. Who could have foreseen, for example, the rapid and permanent shift toward remote work? And who now can truly foresee what long-term impact this shift will have on data flows, automation, and connectivity, to say nothing of its influence on society and the human experience?

We are launching into an era defined by new technologies—artificial intelligence, zero-party data, digital currencies, metaverses, and more. There is no shortage of excitement around the benefits these tools may bring.

But the decisions we make today will have long-lasting implications for business and our collective future. As these emerging and maturing technologies intersect, the results defy prediction. Collisions between these new tools call us to reconsider what we think we know about ethics and trustworthy technology. Reading this book, familiarizing yourself with these developments, and thinking about their impact will set you on the right path.

New Concepts for a New Era

The technologies transforming the world are at different stages of maturity. Non-fungible tokens (NFTs) are relatively new, while AI has matured to deliver value at scale, and in just over a decade, cloud computing has become a 21st-century business necessity. The rapid pace of this evolution challenges us to continuously imagine, anticipate, and address the implications for values and ethics.

It is rarely a straight path from innovation to ethical use that generates real value. When we solve initial challenges, new ones emerge. As we use our new tools, our thinking grows more nuanced on how to do so appropriately and correctly. Sometimes the path doubles back on itself. An illustrative example is our evolving attitude toward data and privacy.

About 20 years ago, when search engines and social media were gaining mass adoption, there was little public awareness of how personal data was used, stored, and sometimes sold. With millions of new users discovering the benefits of connectivity and access to information, and with new interoperabilities and partnerships rolling out constantly, the notion of data privacy was far from top of mind for most internet users. This did not last long. In the years that followed, a sobering realization took hold: "If you are not paying for the product, you are the product."

Soon, business and consumer sentiment swung away from the freewheeling days of data sharing toward privacy. Data collection became fraught with questions around control over one's personal information and the "right to be forgotten." Businesses made privacy-focused policy choices, and government bodies developed regulations and laws around data storage and application.

But that wasn't the end. During the pandemic, the pendulum began to swing back, bringing with it a new paradigm in which privacy remains valuable, but data sharing has commensurate merit. Exchanging data helped researchers develop vaccines and new treatments. Some nations and communities were enthusiastic about contact tracing to help limit the spread of disease. Data sharing—with safeguards in place—saved lives.

This cycle of innovation and ethical questioning can be found throughout the technological fields. We are called to think about not just what these tools can *do* but also what they *mean*—and that meaning may change when they collide with other new innovations. Each technology in this book raises its own host of ethical uncertainties that lead us to ask whether we can (or should) trust the transformative tools reshaping the world around us.

An Inflection Point

Discussions of ethics often include concerns about privacy, the potential for bias, and the transparency of the organization deploying the technology vis-à-vis the end user. These elements are important to address when fostering trust, but they only scratch the surface of the broader concept of trustworthy technology.

Consider automobiles. Drivers expect that their car can reliably start and stop and that it includes safety devices like airbags and security devices like locks and alarms. Modern cars are used in the context of a socio-technical system composed of speed limits, traffic lights, pedestrians, and traffic enforcement. A car can be trusted because of the sum total of these and other elements. Consider how different this modern system is from what existed when the first Model T rolled off the assembly line.

Today's emerging technologies will be even more impactful. Part of the challenge before us is that ethical concerns and expectations vary between communities, geographies, and industries. What is considered trustworthy in one context may be insufficient in another, and what is acceptable at one time may eventually become problematic. For example, when evaluating the trustworthiness of a car today, we must also consider the impact of its emissions on climate—a ramification that was largely unconsidered a few decades ago.

When evaluating the ethics of converging technologies, what's needed is a treatment of the ethics of each component tool, as well as those of the larger ecosystem in which they function. In the business context, this includes designing processes to embed trust as a quality of the technology. This could include, for example, inserting clear waypoints throughout a project for assessing ethics across the AI life cycle. An organization may also look to its workforce and consider whether new roles or skills are required to govern trustworthy AI.

Indeed, the ethics of technology are ultimately as much about the people using the tools as they are about the tools themselves. It is impossible to separate business principles from human morals from the ethical use of technology. Our decisions will determine where the trends take us.

Will the metaverse be a great provider of transparency and equal opportunity, or will it be opaque, its value uneven to its users or, worse, addictive and exploitative? Will workers be empowered by using AI in their tasks? Will contactless commerce change the retail experience for the better? These are questions that we can begin to answer by making business decisions that align with ethical priorities.

A Bright Forecast

The new technologies examined in this book are some of the most powerful tools humanity has devised, with the potential to impact nearly every facet of our lives and work. But this is not the first time we have stood on the threshold of transformation and gazed at a foggy horizon, wondering in what direction our tools might take us—and where we might take them.

History has lessons for us. The development of nuclear fission granted us enormous energy, which has fueled spacecraft to tour the solar system while also leading to catastrophes. The dawn of the internet unleashed knowledge on a scale that dwarfs the impact of even the printing press, but it also created profound issues for security, safety, and privacy.

As you read through this book, look for intersections of technologies that are emerging and that are established in businesses. The first section, "New Fundamentals," examines a handful of technologies that seem futuristic now but are on the cusp of becoming everyday tools. Next, "Fresh Takes on Mature Tech" discusses tools that now seem ordinary—the cloud, cybersecurity, cookies—but require another look now that collisions have brought about new applications and contexts. Section three, "AI for the Rest of Us," focuses on how artificial intelligence is no longer an exotic tool but a democratized one, available to any business. Finally, section four, "Trust Me," reexamines the theme of trustworthy technology with a pair of in-depth cases.

This is a promising new era, and we are right to be optimistic. Our destination with these technologies and how we get there is ours to decide. It will take knowledge and introspection to reach our destination, and the chapters that follow aid us on our journey.

Section 1

NEW FUNDAMENTALS

HOW BRANDS CAN ENTER THE METAVERSE

by Janet Balis

Quite a few people believe that the latest paradigm shift for the internet is well underway: The metaverse, they say, is almost here. When companies investing in a space and the media declare a moment, it's reasonable to take a beat and see whether the reality can live up to the hype. But, if this is *the* "meta" moment—that is, if it offers something that people really want—it is safe to assume that a lot of companies are wondering what the metaverse really is and whether they should be a part of it.

For brands thinking about how to navigate this new frontier, even knowing where to start can be daunting.

The basic idea of the metaverse isn't complicated. Put simply, the metaverse includes any digital experience on the internet that is persistent, immersive, three-dimensional (3D), and virtual, as in, not happening in the physical world. Metaverse experiences offer us the opportunity to play, work, connect, or buy (and just to make things extra fun, the things we buy can be real or virtual). It is also perhaps a misnomer to say "the metaverse" as if it were a monolithic, connected, or even interoperable universe, because it is not. Each entity that creates a virtual world does so with its own access, membership, monetization rights, and formats of creative expression, so the business and technical specifications vary widely. The metaverse refers more to the concept across these individual worlds and experiences and the acknowledgment that we are entering into a more substantive, immersive landscape than before.

A handful of businesses are already shaping the landscape, with entertainment and gaming companies leading the way. Major console and PC gaming titles, such as *Fortnite* from Epic Games, have normalized playing and

---

The views expressed are those of the author and do not necessarily represent the views of Ernst & Young LLP or any other member firm of the global EY organization.

socializing with people in virtual settings. Newer gaming platforms, such as Roblox, allow people to create and play across immersive worlds created, and often monetized, by users. Decentraland is an entire 3D virtual world owned by its users, allowing them to create virtual structures—from theme parks to galleries—and then charge users to visit them, all powered by Ethereum blockchain technology. Other companies, such as MetaVRse and Unity, are creating engines to power brand and gaming studios and accelerate development of AR and VR content creation.

The immersive environment of the metaverse isn't just an opportunity for consumer-facing companies, however. From training future surgeons to rolling out product demos to retail employees, there are plenty of business applications. For example, the leadership of tech company Nvidia believes that investing in metaverse simulations of such things as manufacturing and logistics will reduce waste and accelerate better business solutions. And Microsoft is positioning its cloud services to be the fabric of the metaverse, using its Mesh platform to enable avatars and immersive spaces to thread into the collaboration environments, such as Teams, over time. With hybrid or remote working environments, many of these more creative virtual business experiences will likely be even more relevant to how companies connect to their people and to their customers.

For companies still waiting on the sidelines, each brand must find its place and balance the risk-reward equation. Doing so requires grasping what is possible, and the companies that are leaning in fast can both offer inspiration and act as test cases. For example, plenty of brands are taking full advantage of the gaming part of the metaverse with branded experiences that are essentially virtual and immersive sponsorships. While Nike is a highly established brand, it is certainly leading the charge at the assertive end of the metaverse spectrum, filing for patents for virtual goods and the opportunity to build virtual retail environments to sell those goods.[1] It has acquired a company called RTFKT that creates virtual sneakers and collectibles for the metaverse.

The commercial applications of the metaverse are even further heightened by the new behaviors that are surging around buying products and services directly from social experiences, also known as "social commerce." Social commerce is becoming a larger percentage of U.S. e-commerce over time and was projected to be $36 billion in 2021 alone, following growth patterns like those in China.[2]

In response, the social media landscape is keen to capitalize on the intersection of where people connect and buy not only in a traditional internet context, but also in a 3D, immersive metaverse. Virtual showrooms, fashion shows, and dressing rooms suddenly have the potential to shift from fringe experimentation to mass adoption. And people aren't just selling physical goods—Sotheby's announced its own metaverse gallery for curated virtual art, housed in Decentraland. New business models for influencers, virtual goods—including non-fungible tokens (NFTs), which are one-of-a-kind creations traded and secured on a blockchain—and commerce on physical goods purchased in virtual worlds will all emerge in importance as capabilities scale.

Brands should always be in a test-and-learn mode, and the digital landscape in particular requires intellectual curiosity. The metaverse is potentially the next iteration of how humans use the internet to connect, communicate, and transact—sitting on the sidelines too long is not likely to be an option.

Here's what brands can do right now.

Pick your targets. Think about how much time your target audiences or customers are spending in the metaverse and calibrate your speed of attack appropriately; brands focusing on younger demographics, for example, probably don't have the luxury of sitting out the metaverse for long. Who are your target demographics, and what behaviors are trending with your current and prospective consumers right now that are indicators of how fast to move into the metaverse?

Watch the competition. Start talking about moments when peer companies do things in the metaverse—like a showcase at a leadership meeting—just to get the conversation going across the executive team. So much of the space can be intimidating, particularly when seemingly indecipherable concepts, such as NFTs or blockchain, are involved. Can you create a champion for these topics to bring approachable, tangible examples to every meeting?

Look for applications. See whether the metaverse gives you opportunities as a company not only to try new things, but also to accelerate your purpose or long-term goals like sustainability, which is well suited to many applications of the metaverse. Almost every chief marketing officer already has made, or will soon make, a public commitment to sustainability-related environmental, social, and governance goals, and they will soon be measurable. What can you pilot in the metaverse that allows you to test more sustainable approaches to serving your customers?

Plan your entrance. Ask your agency team to begin formulating a point of view on how your brand should show up in the metaverse and when it might make sense. Holding companies and independent agencies are both keenly watching mass media behaviors and emerging trends, so it's a great opportunity to ask them what they are seeing across their client portfolio. What tests could they put in place to enable you to comfortably expose your brand to the metaverse?

Keep your balance. If you are already in it, prepare for the fact that all new spaces present risk and reward; manage accordingly, knowing that it may be super-unpredictable and lacking in standards. The good news is that the pandemic made us all more agile than before. To state the epically obvious, there will be experiments that fail. Second Life offered the promise of the metaverse years ago and did not take hold, but the risk for the brands that participated was not significant or long term. So, if this is the right time, consider how to be there.

. . .

Most importantly, people in brand marketing or leadership roles should start thinking about how to unleash their creativity and their storytelling. If the creative palette expands dimensions in the metaverse, we should be excited to create experiences at any point in the customer journey, from acquisition to engagement to transaction to customer support, that have the potential to be both spectacular and stickier than before. And, someday, we will likely want to move from real to virtual worlds seamlessly. That will be the next frontier.

TAKEAWAYS

For brands considering entering the metaverse, even knowing where to start can be daunting. But it's risky to sit on the sidelines too long. Follow these guidelines as your brand makes its first plays in this new frontier.

✓ **Pick your targets.** Think about how much time your target audiences are spending in the metaverse and calibrate your speed of attack. If they're already there, you need to ramp up quickly.

✓ **Watch the competition.** Pay attention to when peer companies enter the metaverse and what they're doing there.

✓ **Look for applications.** See whether the metaverse gives you opportunities as a company to not only try new things but also accelerate your purpose or long-term goals.

✓ **Plan your entrance.** Consider tests you could put in place to enable you to comfortably expose your brand to the metaverse.

✓ **Keep your balance.** Expect that the metaverse will be unpredictable and have varying standards.

NOTES

1. Jessica Golden, "Nike Is Quietly Preparing for the Metaverse," CNBC, November 2, 2021, https://www.cnbc.com/2021/11/02/nike-is-quietly-preparing-for-the-metaverse-.html.

2. Andrew Lipsman, "Social Commerce 2021," Insider Intelligence, February 3, 2021, https://www.emarketer.com/content/social-commerce-2021.

Adapted from content posted on hbr.org, January 3, 2022 (product #H06RJ8).

2

HOW NFTs CREATE VALUE

by Steve Kaczynski and Scott Duke Kominers

I n March 2021, a work of art called *Everydays: The First 5000 Days* sold for $69 million at Christie's auction house. It's not out of the ordinary to see eight-figure art sales, but this one received a lot of attention because the piece was sold as a non-fungible token (NFT)—an electronic record corresponding to an image that lives entirely in the digital world.

Put differently: Someone paid almost $70 million for a picture on the internet.

Since then, NFTs have started to permeate pop culture in various ways. They've been spoofed by *Saturday Night*

Live and embraced by high-profile celebrities like rapper Snoop Dogg and NBA superstar Stephen Curry. As of this writing, there are hundreds of millions of dollars of NFT sales each week through public marketplaces like Foundation, OpenSea, and Nifty Gateway, as well as custom-built applications like NBA Top Shot and VeVe.

Yet, at the same time, many people wonder how tokens on the internet could be worth any money at all—especially when many of them just represent "ownership" of an online image or animation that you could, in principle, download a copy of for free.

It's easy to see why NFTs inspire both excitement and deep skepticism: They're a completely novel asset class, and we don't see new asset classes appear that often. But what drives the value of an asset that's really just a digital token people can pass around? To appreciate NFTs properly, we first have to think through what they actually are and the types of market opportunities they enable. And once we unlock that, we can understand how to build businesses around them.

---

aczynski and Kominers own NFTs, as well as other crypto
, Kominers provides market design advice to a number
nesses and crypto projects, including Novi Financial,
ation, koodos, and Quora.

NFTs as a Tool for Market Design

NFTs have fundamentally changed the market for digital assets. Historically there was no way to separate the "owner" of a digital artwork from someone who just saved a copy to their desktop. Markets can't operate without clear property rights: Before someone can buy a good, it has to be clear who has the right to sell it, and once someone does buy, you need to be able to transfer ownership from the seller to the buyer. NFTs solve this problem by giving parties something they can agree represents ownership. In doing so, they make it possible to build markets around new types of transactions—buying and selling products that could never be sold before or enabling transactions to happen in innovative ways that are more efficient and valuable.

Each NFT is a unique, one-of-a-kind digital item. They're stored on public-facing digital ledgers called blockchains, which means it's possible to prove who owns a given NFT at any moment in time and trace the history of prior ownership. Moreover, it's easy to transfer NFTs from one person to another—just as a bank might move money across accounts—and it's very hard to counterfeit them. Because NFT ownership is easy to certify and transfer, we can use them to create markets in a variety of different goods.

But NFTs don't just provide a kind of digital "deed." Because blockchains are programmable, it's possible to endow NFTs with features that enable them to expand their purpose over time, or even to provide direct utility to their holders. In other words, NFTs can do things—or let their owners do things—in both digital spaces and the physical world.

In this sense, NFTs can function like membership cards or tickets, providing access to events, exclusive merchandise, and special discounts—as well as serving as digital keys to online spaces where holders can engage with each other. Moreover, because the blockchain is public, it's even possible to send additional products directly to anyone who owns a given token. All of this gives NFT holders value over and above simple ownership—and provides creators with a vector to build a highly engaged community around their brands.

It's not uncommon to see creators organize in-person meetups for their NFT holders. In other cases, having a specific NFT in your online wallet might be necessary in order to gain access to an online game, chat room, or merchandise store. And creator teams sometimes grant additional tokens to their NFT holders in ways that expand the product ecosystem: Owners of a particular goat NFT, for example, were able to claim a free baby goat NFT that gives benefits beyond the original token; holders of a particular bear NFT, meanwhile, just received honey.

Thus, owning an NFT effectively makes you an investor, a member of a club, a brand shareholder, and a participant in a loyalty program all at once. At the same time, NFTs' programmability supports new business and profit models; for example, NFTs have enabled a new type of royalty contract, whereby each time a work is resold, a share of the transaction goes back to the original creator.

This all means that NFT-based markets can emerge and gain traction quickly, especially relative to other crypto products. This is both because the NFTs themselves have stand-alone value—you might buy an art NFT simply because you like it—and because NFTs just need to establish value among a community of potential owners (which can be relatively small), whereas cryptocurrencies need wide acceptance in order to become useful as a store of value or medium of exchange.

The Advent of NFT Ecosystems

As marketplaces have sprung up around NFTs, creators have taken advantage of their possibilities in different ways.

The best-known examples are the digital art market, already described, and digital collectibles platforms, such as Dapper Labs's NBA Top Shot, which enables users to collect and exchange NFTs of exciting plays from basketball games—videos called "moments," which are effectively digital trading cards. Top Shot has been building in gamified challenges and other reasons to own the cards beyond just their pure collectible value, even teasing that moment holders may eventually receive real-world benefits from the NBA.

But what's emerged more recently is a model of active ecosystem-building around NFT-native properties, leading to novel organizations developed entirely within the NFT space. These products start with an NFT series, but project forward a road map under which holders of the NFT gain access to an expanding array of products, activities, and experiences. Revenue from initial and subsequent NFT sales is fed back into the brand, supporting increasingly ambitious projects, which in turn drive up the value of the NFTs themselves.

The Bored Ape Yacht Club, for example, comprises a series of NFT ape images conferring membership in an online community. The project started with a series of private chat rooms and a graffiti board and has grown to include high-end merchandise, social events, and even an actual yacht party. SupDucks and the Gutter Cat Gang similarly began building communities around NFT image series and associated online spaces; the former has bridged into a boardwalk-themed metaverse game, and the latter has focused on real-world benefits like extravagant in-person events.

People often take on membership in these collectives as part of their personal identity, even using their favorite NFT image as their public profile picture on social media. Each NFT community has different personalities and purposes, and there are so many that almost everyone can find a group they can call their own. In this way, NFT ownership provides an immediate shared text that people can use to connect with each other.

Moreover, in many of these communities, ownership also conveys partial or full commercial rights—or even some degree of governance in how the community is run—which means members can build properties on top of their NFTs that grow the value of the overall brand. Crucially, this creates a channel by which engaged fandom can feed back into the brand itself: "Jenkins the Valet" is a Bored Ape member-created project that has effectively become its own sub-brand. Individual SupDucks members have created art and character identities around their NFTs that have been absorbed into the SupDucks metaverse. And community-created fan projects have built out parts of the Gutter Cat Gang story arc.

All of these benefits make owning the associated NFTs more valuable, and almost paradoxically, this increase in the value of ownership comes in a form that helps separate the value of ownership from the purely financial opportunity of reselling.

Building on this phenomenon, a few well-known brands have recently introduced NFT series that serve to identify, reinforce, and expand their existing communities of brand enthusiasts. The popular streetwear brand The Hundreds, for example, has built an NFT project around its mascot the "Adam Bomb" and directly rewards its community of NFT holders with improved access to the brand through connection with the founders and early access to new product releases.

Many emerging NFT applications, meanwhile, are seeking to more explicitly blend online NFT ownership with offline use cases. A few restaurants, for example, have started using NFTs for reservations. And the ticketing industry has a major opportunity here: By issuing tickets as NFTs, venues can give a variety of benefits to purchasers, creating more incentive to buy and providing the venues an opportunity to collect royalties on secondary sales.

Other companies are exploring how to use NFTs in establishing and recording people's identity and reputation online. MIT recently started offering blockchain-based digital diplomas, which are effectively nontransferable NFTs. Meanwhile, both established players like Meta and new ventures like POAP and koodos are providing ways for individuals to create and share NFTs around activities, affinities, and interests.

How These Businesses Can Succeed

Like all other businesses, each NFT project has to respond to a real market need. But there are unique challenges to building in the NFT space.

They must make meaningful use of the NFT technology itself

It's not an accident that so many of the early NFT projects are built around digital rights management, because that's one of the most direct applications of the technology. Club membership benefits for NFT holders fit in naturally as well, since a given NFT holder can certify their right to have access simply by pointing to the token in their crypto wallet.

But NFTs make less sense when there isn't a purpose to digital ownership, such as for managing physical collectibles, where people presumably want to receive the objects themselves. (Unless, of course, they're too heavy to move, as in the case of an NFT for a 2,000-pound tungsten cube.)

NFTs have to leverage a community of users

As with any new product, early adopters serve as product evangelists and a source of early feedback. But with NFTs, these users also serve an even more essential role: Their decision to embrace the NFTs quite literally imbues those NFTs with their meaning and establishes their initial value.

Without a robust community of users, NFT projects can fail to get off the ground, or can quickly collapse as all the token holders lose interest. And this means that if an NFT project doesn't make its value proposition clear enough at the outset, it can fail to recruit a big enough community—or the right community. Lack of engagement can then become a self-fulfilling prophecy, devaluing the NFTs themselves.

To maintain ongoing community engagement, NFT project teams must generate confidence that they can continue executing

In the world of crypto, where many people engage partially or completely anonymously, crises of confidence in a project can cascade quickly, which means it's particularly important that the team communicate frequently and transparently about how they intend to evolve the project. (Many NFT teams have frequent "community calls" for this purpose.)

Here NFT projects can also lean on established brands or institutions, as well as explicit promises of real-world utility. For example, a sports team or popular music artist selling tickets through NFTs can use their existing reputation and events infrastructure to convince people that the NFT tickets really do have value. That said, an existing company releasing an NFT without any specific purpose or value can look gimmicky and thus fail to create engagement.

NFT projects need on-ramps for new users

NFTs also face a number of challenges that are general across crypto entrepreneurship. Most crypto technology at the moment is not user-friendly to engage with, requiring interfacing with a number of abstruse cryptocurrency exchanges and wallet providers.

NBA Top Shot has benefited tremendously from submerging most of the underlying crypto structure in its NFT market and enabling users to purchase moments in fiat with credit cards, rather than requiring people to transact in cryptocurrency. Other projects have recruited onboarding directors to help first-time NFT consumers navigate the process of purchasing.

NFT projects need to be able to weather crypto market swings

Additionally, crypto markets are volatile, and the surrounding regulatory frameworks are still being sorted out. These market swings can dramatically change the demand for NFTs, which again underscores the importance of building community and other sources of direct value for NFT ownership.

Outlook

As with any novel asset class, the future of NFTs is uncertain. In the long run, the market will need to contend with the transaction and environmental costs currently associated with using crypto technology. We will also need to establish more explicit legal frameworks around NFT ownership and clarify how NFTs relate to existing forms of ownership rights, especially around intellectual property. At the same time, it's likely that the most valuable applications of NFTs haven't even been envisioned yet.

Nevertheless, the community-based NFT projects that have taken off so far hint at what may be to come.

NFTs enable new markets by allowing people to create and build upon new forms of ownership. These projects succeed by leveraging a core dynamic of crypto: A token's worth comes from users' shared agreement, and this means that the community one builds around NFTs quite literally creates those NFTs' underlying value. And the more these communities increase engagement and become part of people's personal identities, the more that value is reinforced.

Newer applications will take greater advantage of online–off-line connections and introduce increasingly complex token designs. But it's less surprising than you might think that people are making money selling pictures on the internet.

TAKEAWAYS

Amid a flood of new NFT ventures, it can be hard to tell which have merit and which are just riding the hype. But there is a logic to how—and when—they create value. Companies that have been most successful in this new frontier are able to:

- ✓ **Make meaningful use of the NFT technology itself.** NFTs make less sense when there isn't a purpose to digital ownership (such as managing physical collectibles).

- ✓ **Leverage a community of users.** Lack of engagement can become a self-fulfilling prophecy, devaluing the NFTs themselves.

- ✓ **Generate confidence that they can continue executing.** Teams must communicate frequently and transparently about how they intend to evolve the project.

- ✓ **Offer on-ramps for new users.** "Submerging" crypto technology allows new users to engage with NFTs more easily.

- ✓ **Stay resilient amid crypto market swings.** Price volatility and an evolving regulatory framework are inevitable.

Adapted from content posted on hbr.org, November 10, 2021 (product #H06OR1).

3

STABLECOINS AND THE FUTURE OF MONEY

by Christian Catalini and Jai Massari

I n late 2021, U.S. Securities and Exchange Commission Chair Gary Gensler made a strong statement: It's time to regulate cryptocurrency markets. He is not the only regulator who believes this. Jerome Powell, chair of the Federal Reserve, issued an urgent call for regulation of stablecoins—cryptocurrencies that are pegged to a reference asset such as the U.S. dollar—and Federal Reserve Governor Lael Brainard signaled that the case for the Federal Reserve to explore a central bank digital currency (CBDC) in response to stablecoins seems to be getting stronger.

Regulators typically only pay this level of attention to systemically important segments of the financial system, such as banks and money market funds. These statements add to a growing body of evidence that unlike cryptocurrencies like Bitcoin and Ethereum—which widely fluctuate in value—stablecoins have the potential to play an important (if yet to be defined) role in the future of global finance. They could even become a backbone for payments and financial services.

To state the obvious, this means that major changes might be afoot for central banks, regulators, and the financial sector. These changes could bring a host of benefits, but also new and very real risks.

To economists, the benefits of stablecoins include lower-cost, safe, real-time, and more competitive payments compared to what consumers and businesses experience today. They could rapidly make it cheaper for businesses to accept payments and easier for governments to run conditional cash transfer programs (including sending stimulus money). They could connect unbanked or underbanked segments of the population to the financial system. But without robust legal and economic frameworks, there's a real risk stablecoins would be anything but stable. They could collapse like an unsound currency board, "break the buck" like money market funds in 2008, or spiral into worthlessness. They could replicate the turmoil of the "wildcat" banks of the 19th century.

While the pros and cons of stablecoins may be debatable, their rise isn't. The question is what should be done about them—and who should be responsible for doing it. Responses range from arguing that the current system is fine, to accelerating research into CBDCs, to emphasizing that stablecoins may be a natural evolution of the combination of public and private money that we have relied on for centuries. While it is hard to defend a system where 15% of U.S. adults in the bottom 40% of the income distribution are unbanked and where low-income account holders—particularly Black and Hispanic customers— pay more than $12 a month for basic access to the financial system, it is also clear that new technology can bring new risks.

Making major changes to how money works is complex, but governments do not have to tackle this all at once. In fact, such an approach is unlikely to succeed. The public sector, both in the United States and elsewhere in the world, has not been particularly successful in deploying digital services. (China is the exception here: As of this writing, it has already cleared over $5.3 billion in transactions through its digital renminbi.) But there are also risks with private-sector involvement, especially as stablecoins move beyond cryptocurrency trading and decentralized finance. Any solution would need to address consumer protection, financial stability, and financial crime prevention. These are the same concerns we always face in the provision of money.

So how should central banks and regulators respond? There are three simple ways we could "upgrade" money that play to the strength of both the public and private sectors. They're different but not mutually exclusive, and each presents significant opportunities for existing financial institutions, as well as fintech and crypto entrants. These opportunities will continue to drive partnerships between established and new players, but also will result in fiercer competition.

Upgrading Money

Modern money is a combination of public and private money. Public money includes central banks–issued cash and digital claims against central banks. Private money includes deposit claims against commercial banks. While the public sector protects the stability of money, up to 95% of money in developed economies is private.

Stablecoins are a form of private money. This is not a new concept; the idea of separating monetary and credit functions traces back 80 years. By lowering the cost of digital verification, blockchain technology can expand the role of both the public and private sectors in the provision of money. While the public sector could attempt to connect with consumers and businesses directly, the private sector is likely to be more efficient in meeting the public's needs and increasing choice.

Succeeding in this transformation will require the right balance between the public and private sectors. Countries that overemphasize the public approach will likely end up falling short in speed to market, competition, and innovation. They will also be unable to nurture the fintech players of the future. The history of the internet is instructive—countries that harnessed the technology's "powerful commercial engine" came out ahead—and the history of financial markets is, too: Countries without robust regulatory frameworks may see under-reserved "wildcat stablecoins" and a race to the bottom on consumer protection.

Consistent with the history of modern money, there is high option value in allowing for experimentation between competing approaches. Public and private experiments are strong complements here, not substitutes. Technology-neutral regulation that follows a "same risks, same rules" approach can lift quality standards and encourage competition between safe solutions.

Different solutions will present different challenges in terms of how they may accelerate the unbundling of payments, credit, and financial services. While such unbundling is eventually inevitable, we're already starting to see how different approaches might play out. By deploying the digital renminbi, China is the first country to make a bold statement about the future of global payments and the type of data the government should have access to. It is now on other countries, particularly the United States in its role as keeper of the world's reserve currency, to develop their own thesis of what that future should look like, and what role they play.

Three Paths to Sound Money

Having spent three years working through these issues and collecting feedback from regulators, we believe there are three ways to safely harness the technology: "true" stablecoins, deposit coins, and CBDCs.

True stablecoins

True stablecoins are non-interest-bearing coins designed to have stable value against a reference currency—say

US$1. Stability is achieved through two commitments. First, the issuer agrees to mint and buy back coins at par. Second, the issuer holds assets to back its obligation to redeem the outstanding stablecoins. This reserve provides comfort that the issuer can buy back all outstanding coins, on demand. Reserve assets should be denominated in the currency of the reference asset, remain highly liquid during a crisis, and incur extremely small losses in a run or stressed market conditions.

True stablecoins are a variation on the concept of narrow banks. They should hold 100% reserves in high-quality, liquid assets—like U.S. Treasuries or cash at the Federal Reserve—against their coin liabilities, plus an additional capital cushion against operational losses, asset price declines, or a run. Like narrow banks, true stablecoins should not engage in maturity transformation. Furthermore, they should isolate reserve assets from their other assets, so that in insolvency or bankruptcy, coin holders can be prioritized over other creditors.

As with narrow banks, the economic benefits of true stablecoins may be . . . narrow. It is expensive to hold full reserves at scale. While capital requirements for state trust banks may be compatible with a full reserve approach, Office of the Comptroller of the Currency (OCC) national trust banks currently face leverage ratios of 4%

to 5%, and therefore may not be a viable structure for issuers that do not engage in maturity transformation.

Even with these limitations, however, true stablecoins have utility as a medium of exchange. They would be optimized for efficiently moving value as opposed to storing value or earning interest. Their cost structure makes them viable when their coin velocity is high and can support a large volume of payments with a small reserve. When it comes to store of value, deposit coins have an advantage, as they have a much lower cost of capital.

Deposit (stable)coins

Deposit stablecoins are demand deposit claims against insured commercial banks, on blockchain rails. They represent an amount a person holds on deposit with an insured bank and therefore an unsecured deposit liability of that bank. Holders are protected by the legal framework governing deposits, including bank capital requirements and FDIC insurance up to $250,000.

Deposit coins combine the benefits of real-time (possibly) lower-cost payments and new functionality with FDIC deposit insurance protection. A bank can use deposit coin proceeds for a wide variety of purposes, including lending. Thus deposit coins keep payments and maturity transformation activities bundled.

Like improvements to existing systems, deposit coins preserve the status quo and keep the system of private money, payments, and banking intertwined. But they also suffer similar limitations.

Absent new technology and legal infrastructure, deposit coins may not be fully interoperable. Each holder would need to be onboarded by the issuing bank, and transfers between different deposit coins would have to be supported by intrabank liquidity and infrastructure, in the same way that ACH and Fedwire support deposit payments.

The interoperability challenges, however, are likely to be temporary. The larger limitation is that only depository institutions can offer deposit coins and that fully backed models are not commercially viable without adjustments to capital requirements. Indeed, it is unclear why a depository institution would ever issue a true stablecoin over a deposit coin.

Central bank digital currencies

To be truly transformative, CBDCs need to bring the benefits of cash on more efficient digital rails and could represent the public sector's response to decreasing demand for physical cash.

In the United States, those who have access to banks, debit cards, credit cards, and digital wallets tend to think of those forms of money as cash. But they aren't; they are liabilities of their private-sector issuers. Cash is a liability of the central bank. While there is digital, central bank money in the United States already, only financial institutions can access it.

A CBDC would make digital cash available to the public. A vibrant debate is taking place about whether a digital dollar is necessary, useful, or even sensible. The answer largely depends on key design decisions about how the CBDC is distributed, to whom it is made available, and whether it should carry an interest rate.

If a CBDC is distributed only through Federal Reserve members, the solution would have similar reach and trade-offs as deposit coins. And it would place the Federal Reserve in competition with its members. The tension arises because a CBDC would be the safest asset available. Without adjustments such as balance limits (for example, the FDIC insurance limit) or zero or negative interest on CBDC balances, consumers might rationally choose a CBDC over bank deposits.

Even a well-designed CBDC that addresses these risks, is made available to everyone at a low cost, and can be used for instantaneous payments has the potential to be disruptive for providers that rely on high fees. While these fees may have to come down eventually anyway, a CBDC would accelerate the unbundling of credit and payment services.

The public sector may also struggle with serving citizens and businesses effectively. Given the incredibly high bar in terms of resilience and security, it will likely take years for a CBDC to be developed and adopted. Of course, the Chinese example may well prove to be the exception to this rule.

This is where CBDCs and stablecoins are strong complements, not substitutes. The public sector could focus on issuing digital coins and delivering on sound money, while the private sector could build rails and applications. Competition with legacy networks would further ensure a higher degree of resilience and innovation.

Simple Fixes for a Complex Problem

True stablecoins, deposit coins, and CBDCs could each deliver on what economists Gary Gorton of the Yale School of Management and Jeffery Zhang of the Board of Governors of the Federal Reserve System refer to as "no questions asked" money. Any material legal uncertainty for true stablecoins could be addressed by incremental changes to existing law. As currently being considered, true stablecoin regulation should include requirements for permissible reserve assets and for the issuer to honor direct redemption claims, and limits on risky maturity transformation activities. Laws that bolster reserve segregation and coin-holder claims in bankruptcy or insolvency should be considered. Through a sensible regulatory approach, true stablecoins can fulfill their promise without introducing new risks.

The question for central banks and regulators then becomes which combination of the three approaches can also improve competition, lower cost, and increase access to the financial system. While it may be tempting to preserve the status quo, such an approach is unlikely to deliver the same benefits.

Blockchain technology can reshape market structure and improve competition. CBDC rails are one way to achieve this and may be the only way to ensure that consumers have direct access to central bank money. But CBDCs are unlikely to come to market quickly, and there is a high chance that they will be more limited in functionality and programmability.

A much stronger combination would be the public sector focusing on regulation of stablecoins first and then on CBDC issuance on multiple rails later to complement potential shortcomings. Countries that follow this hybrid model and focus on clear risks and market failures are more likely to actually meet consumer and business needs faster and see a new generation of financial institutions thrive within their borders. Interoperability across different rails, privacy, and identity are areas where private-sector incentives may not be aligned with broader societal goals. Public-sector guidance and standard setting can be incredibly useful in promoting the right solutions in these areas.

While it may be tempting to label blockchain technology as yet another instance of "software eating the world," regulatory frameworks will define if and when the technology can deliver on its potential. In the case of money, the public and private sectors can play to their relative strengths, solidify their public-private partnership, and improve societal outcomes in the process.

TAKEAWAYS

While cryptocurrencies such as Bitcoin and Ethereum wildly fluctuate in value, stablecoins have the potential to play an important role in the future of global finance.

There are three stablecoin approaches that have serious potential to affect our system of money:

- ✓ **True stablecoins:** Non-interest-bearing coins designed to have stable value against a reference currency

- ✓ **Deposit coins:** Demand deposit claims against insured commercial banks, on digital rails

- ✓ **Central bank digital currencies:** Cash on digital rails, representing the public sector's response to decreasing demand for physical cash

Adapted from content posted on hbr.org, August 10, 2021 (product #H06ITL).

4

THE FUTURE OF CONTACTLESS COMMERCE

by Mark Purdy

C hoosing the right suit or dress online can be very difficult. There's size, fit, price, color, feel, overall look, and a host of other factors that must be considered. It may look great in the online catalog, but how will it wear in practice? The large volumes of online returns most retailers face suggest that this is not an easy task.

It's not just clothing that's difficult to fully assess online. Fresh food, beverages, cars, perfumes, and furniture are all items we want to sense, test, and try out before making the final purchase decision. In other cases—for example, taking out a mortgage or choosing a bottle of wine—we are often looking for guidance in choosing a complex service or product. While we can turn to any number of product reviews online, they are rarely a substitute for a trusted human adviser who can pierce the informational haze and help us make an informed decision.

The Covid-19 pandemic—and the social distancing it required—presented the ultimate test for many of these fundamental aspects of the customer experience: no fitting rooms, no contact with retail agents, no cash payments, and no in-store testing of products. Retailers learned an important lesson: We need faster, safer, and better in-store experiences that retain and enhance the important elements of closeness and interactivity with products, agents, and the store environment.

This is where next-generation digital technologies can make a massive impact, enabling new forms of "contactless commerce." Contactless commerce can take various forms: a fitting-room mirror that automatically displays the clothing items you've just selected from the racks, or a virtual fashion adviser on your phone who whispers advice on the season's latest fashions. Contactless commerce is being enabled by a wide range of new technologies, including machine learning, robotics, computer vision, sensors, big-data analytics, augmented reality, and computer-aided holography. It is set to transform all elements of the customer experience, from product comparison to selection to checkout.

Seamless Digital Transactions

Radio-frequency-identification (RFID) tags play a major role in the automation of store checkouts. RFID tags, as their name suggests, are tiny strips of metal material that can transmit radio waves with detailed information about the product they are attached to. Imagine a tag that can store a wide array of information about a product—its brand, price, size, color, location in store, other varieties, and inventory levels—and convey that to shoppers and store managers. This is in essence what an RFID tag does. This information can be decoded via a mobile scanner (handheld or attached to a shopping cart, for example) or at a fixed station or kiosk. While RFID tags have been around for at least 20 years in various forms, the key innovation has been the development of very lightweight, disposable strips suitable for use on retail products.

Unlike barcode labels, which an employee or the customer must laboriously scan one at a time, RFID tags not only hold more information, but can be automatically scanned together, vastly accelerating the automatic checkout process. Dirty Lemon, a beverage brand, has used RFID technology to automate the sale of beverages in its New York store: Customers simply take their preferred beverages from the coolers, wave the item under a reader to get product details, and then pay by text message, either in store or after they leave.

Using a somewhat different technology mix, Amazon Go has developed Just Walk Out technology for its own stores and a number of retail clients. With the aid of sensors and computer vision, the store can track when consumers physically take an item from the shelf or return it, adding it or taking it away from a virtual cart. The customer can just walk out with their chosen items, which are automatically scanned and charged to the customer's account. (The customer can use a QR code from the Amazon app to enter the just-walk-out gates, or they can insert any credit card at the gates if they don't have the app, so they don't need an app or account set up.) Chinese retail giant JD.com has pioneered line-free technology in its stores in China and Indonesia, and a raft of technology startups are also active in this space. Customers avoid the irritation of long lines, while retailers benefit from better monitoring of stock flows and freeing up staff to focus on more valuable tasks such as store management or customer service.

The impact is not confined to automatic checkouts. With RFID tags, every object in a store can potentially interact with the customer. Pointing a reader at a product, mannequin, or display rack can bring up a raft of information about the product range, brand, price, availability, and other features. Many retailers are now introducing interactive fitting rooms where customers can try on items virtually. Japanese retail giant Uniqlo was one of the first to introduce virtual fitting rooms, pioneering its Magic Mirror at its store in San Francisco. Customers can stand in front of an AI-enabled mirror and see an image of themselves wearing the product, with options to vary style, size, color, and patterns. Sephora has trialed augmented reality makeup mirrors in its store in Milan to help customers find the right hue and shade of eye shadow. TriMirror, a Canadian technology company, has brought another dimension to virtual clothes fitting, developing a 3D interactive avatar that models the items for the customer, who can then check for fit in different garment locations and customize the item as desired.

A Feast for the Senses

The retail experience at its best should be a richly varied sensory experience: the opportunity to taste, smell, and touch products, whether that's freshly baked bread, vintage wines, or newly roasted coffee beans. This would seem to present a major hurdle to the digital world of contactless commerce.

Yet, even here, major advances are taking place in the digital recreation and transmission of sensory information. Take the sense of touch. The touch screen—on the ATM, vending machine, railway ticket dispenser, or airport check-in stand—has become the staple interface for customer automation, but also raises the risks of virus and pathogen transmission. One intriguing solution is the AI-enabled "predictive touch" technology developed by researchers at the University of Cambridge. Developed for in-car navigation systems, the technology uses machine learning and data from sensor-tracked eye and finger movements to predict the numerals and letters the user is likely to input, without actually touching the screen. While still at an early stage, the technology could hold great promise for touchless applications across a range of sectors. It takes us closer to a world of gesture recognition, where a wave, a smile, or a frown allows consumers to access and interact with digital screens, products, and electronic objects.

The opportunities don't stop there, however. Advances in digital olfaction increasingly enable the detection and transmission of a wide variety of aromas, from perfumes to fresh food to new car interiors. Researchers are also beginning to unravel the mysteries of how to digitally transmit taste sensations. One promising development is the "lickable screen" developed by scientists at Meiji University in Japan. Customers use a sushi-roll-shaped device that has electrodes immersed in five narrow liquid wells representing the five traditional tastes—salty, sour, bitter, sweet, and umami (or savory). By turning on and off various electrical signals, the device can digitally transmit flavors electronically. While still nascent, the technology opens up the possibility that in the future, your smartphone could become a way to sample flavors in a contactless way, either in store or online.

Pay by Face or Voice

Contactless commerce is also being enabled by AI-powered analysis of biometric data. In the food and beverage industry, the drive-through and corner kiosk are being reinvented for an automated, contactless experience. California-based PopID uses a cloud-based facial-recognition technology to give customers a "pay by face" option when ordering at kiosks or drive-through stations; its technology is already being used by restaurant chains such as CaliBurger, Bojangles, and Dairi-O. Another technology of great potential is voice genomics—

the AI-enabled analysis of vocal tones, patterns, pitch, and timbre. Voice-enabled AI is now being used for automatic customer interaction in a variety of settings. One problem, however, is that automated kiosks and touch screens are often located in noisy locations, such as railway station concourses, which can make voice identification difficult. A potential solution has been developed by Touchless.ai, a technology startup based in Israel, which uses machine-learning algorithms to screen out ambient noise and allow voice-enabled, touchless interaction with kiosks in railways, hospitals, and other noisy locations.

The use of biometric data for contactless commerce may raise concerns—for example, around data security or privacy—which could deter some customers from using the technology. In addition to using opt-in provisions, providers typically have a battery of safeguards in place to reassure customers, for example, by using biometric data only for the current transaction or not storing data beyond a defined period of time.

An Agent at Your Shoulder

The retail experience, of course, is also about curation, advice, help, and support—elements that are harder to provide in a low-contact world. Help is increasingly at hand, however, from a range of AI-powered recommendation systems and virtual agents. French supermarket giant Carrefour has partnered with Google Assistant to provide a voice-enabled online grocery shopping service where the AI features enable the system to learn the customer's shopping habits and make recommendations based on their preferences—for example, for organic or low-fat foods—and factors such as price and availability. For wine aficionados, California-based sensory sciences company Tastry provides personalized wine recommendations based on machine-learning analysis of the chemical composition of thousands of wines from all over the United States. These are matched to user preferences for different varietals, tasting notes, and wine structure.

Further ahead, holographic technology could be a game changer, enabling highly realistic and interactive consumer experiences in a safe and socially distanced manner. Unlike virtual reality technology, which relies on headsets to create an optical illusion of 3D space, holograms are actual recreations of refracted light that can be seen by anyone, without a headset. This gives them a more natural feel and avoids the eyestrain and headaches that can result from prolonged VR exposure. Holographic technology also increasingly incorporates elements of touch and interactivity, giving users the ability to move among people and objects. With computer-generated holography, it is possible to imagine a transformed consumer experience: browsing a virtual bookshop; meeting a holographic mortgage broker to walk through documents; or having a holographic "fashion whisperer" by your side as you try on items in a virtual store.

Imperatives for Success

Contactless commerce brings many opportunities—safer, faster, and content-rich immersive experiences—but it also brings challenges related to privacy, data security, escalating customer expectations, and new roles for in-store staff, to name but a few. To capitalize on the opportunities and mitigate the risks, retailers can consider several actions:

1. **Capture the time dividend.** The increased use of automated, contactless technology will give time back to customers and retailers, but how will they spend that time? Customers could either grab those time savings for other areas of their busy lives or decide to spend more time in store on the more enjoyable parts of the shopping experience, such as exploring new products, socializing with friends, engaging with in-store entertainment, or getting broader lifestyle support. A key factor will

be the extent to which retailers can create immersive, content-rich experiences that are highly personalized for individual consumers.

2. **Follow the customer.** In the world of contactless commerce, we will see a blurring of physical stores and online experiences, as consumers increasingly use AI-powered technology to make choices and purchases across different platforms—voice, mobile, online, and store-based. The entire customer journey will begin to open up, with interactive elements in the conventional "dead zone" between the home and the store. Consider, for example, the interactive advertising used by Battersea Dogs and Cats Home in the UK, a leading animal welfare charity whose mission is to find homes for abandoned pets. Shoppers at a major shopping center in London were handed RFID-enabled leaflets that lit up interactive billboards on their way home, with a prospective pet featured in each. The initiative significantly boosted adoption rates for the charity.

3. **Reinvent the store.** Whether it's a grocery chain, a fast-food restaurant, or a department store, most retailers have detailed planograms or store layouts designed to ease the flow of customers through the store and optimize the shopping experience:

window displays, eye-catching offers up front, es-
sentials further in, all leading inexorably to the
checkout point. In a contactless world, the nature
and function of the store will change dramatically:
It will become a space festooned with interactive
displays and kiosks, virtual reality zones, and an
array of robotic helpers, with fulfillment done from
off-site warehouses or direct to the customer.

From electric lighting to the elevator, from the cash
register to self-service scanners, technology has been a
constant force for innovation in retail. For customers entering the newly opened department stores in Paris and
New York a century and a half ago, the newest form of
commerce was a marvel: illuminated window displays,
mechanized tube delivery systems, tearooms to meet
friends, and endless tracts of store space to roam and explore. With the static shop counter gone, shopping was
transformed from a burdensome chore to an opportunity for discovery and adventure. Spurred by the pandemic, but with a technology-driven momentum of its
own, the coming shift to contactless commerce will be
no less transformative, blending physical and virtual experiences and bringing new types of sensory experiences
and customer-product interactions. Now is the time for

businesses and consumers alike to seize the opportunities of the contactless era.

TAKEAWAYS

The pandemic taught retailers that we need faster, safer, and better in-store experiences that retain and enhance the important elements of closeness and interactivity. Next-generation digital technologies can make a massive impact, enabling new forms of "contactless commerce."

✓ RFID tags could potentially allow any object in a store to interact with customers.

✓ Major advances are taking place in the digital re-creation and transmission of sensory information including touch, smell, and taste.

✓ Biometrics including pay by face and pay by voice are emerging at retailers.

✓ AI-powered recommendation systems and virtual agents are beginning to offer curation, advice, help, and support in the low-contact world.

✓ Retailers should learn how to capture the time consumers save, find ways to reach customers in the "dead zone" between store and home, and reinvent the organization and flow of their stores.

Adapted from content posted on hbr.org, November 22, 2021 (product #H06PDO).

5

HOW TO ATTRACT TOP TECH TALENT

by Jonathan Frick, KC George, and Julie Coffman

The war for technology talent is getting fiercer, with software and technology becoming mission-critical for businesses throughout the economy. It's no longer just tech companies competing against one another for candidates; other industries have jumped into the fray and are winning a larger share of tech talent.

This trend has been underway for a while, but it's accelerating. In 2019, before the Covid-19 pandemic disrupted hiring for most companies, at least temporarily, more than 40% of software engineer and developer hires were made by nontech companies, up from about a third in 2010, according to Bain & Company's analysis of U.S. data.

Even as demand from nontech companies grows, many companies are struggling to compete for top talent because the largest technology companies and tech startups are sucking up top-flight candidates at unprecedented rates. Over the past decade, they have been increasing the size of their software engineering and developer staffs by nearly 60% each year, the fastest hiring pace among tech and nontech companies, according to our analysis.

The emerging winners recognize that the key to overcoming the talent crunch is to widen their funnel of candidates by seeking those with a broader set of desired capabilities—not only technical skills—from a much more diverse pool. Mastery of technical skills remains critical, especially for roles where software coding prowess is paramount, but technical skills are less crucial for some tech roles, including fast-growing jobs such as customer success and product managers. Focusing on a wider set of capabilities germane to each role can open up a larger pool of desirable candidates. Companies taking this approach recognize that if they find a person who possesses the capabilities most predictive of success in the role—for example, collaboration, stress management, and self-confidence in the case of customer success managers—the new hire can learn the rest on the job through training (both formal and informal).

The art of effectively doing this kind of search depends on developing systematic processes to mitigate bias (conscious or unconscious) across the talent-acquisition and management organizations. At Airbnb, beyond giving recruiters and interviewers unconscious-bias training, hiring managers start by thinking through the objective criteria and must-have attributes for a role. Then, they define specific rubrics that align with the desired skills to minimize bias in hiring.

To win their desired candidates, leading companies don't just implement measures that job seekers now consider table stakes, such as a strong company mission and purpose, competitive pay and benefits packages, and a track record of investing in training and career path opportunities. These firms also create differentiators that help them beat out competitors for the most sought-after talent, including the millennials and members of Generation Z who make up a growing share of the workforce.

Based on Bain's analysis of Glassdoor ratings of tech companies, three factors are emerging as strong influences on where the most talented candidates want to work.

1. Commitment to Diversity and Inclusion

Recruiting a diverse and inclusive workforce is the right thing to do, and its positive effects on business performance are well documented. Plus, a strong diversity, equity, and inclusion (DEI) strategy can help companies attract talent because it has become an important factor in recruits' decision-making. In a Beqom survey of 1,000 employed adults in 2020, 48% said they'd consider switching to another company if it had a built-out DEI strategy. But companies really have no choice if they want to overcome the tech talent crunch; ignoring a huge swath of the talent pool isn't an option.

The good news is that opening the recruiting aperture beyond typical sources of recruits helps here, too. Objectively testing for capabilities and skills rather than relying on past experience and credentials has been shown to improve diversity as well. For example, more companies are recognizing that they can find excellent software engineering candidates by scouting recruits with coding boot camp certificates and highly rated coding work samples on GitHub, regardless of whether the candidate has a computer science degree from a prestigious university. That approach opens up more opportunities for underrepresented candidates and widens the company's talent funnel.

2. Transparent and Accountable Senior Management

At high-performing tech companies, managers are usually visible and willing to engage directly with employees. They also act with speed and decisiveness, and hold themselves accountable for real outcomes. For example, Slack, the business communication and collaboration software maker, created an internal #exec-ama ("ask me anything") chat channel. Employees can ask anything of the executive team, and executives are expected to (and actually do) respond.

The best talent, of course, will prefer a firm where they feel their work has real impact. If employees feel leadership is intransigent and unaccountable, they're more likely to leave to build a competing company.

3. Culture of Coaching and Development

The path to creating a winning culture can seem opaque, but one clear enabler is high-quality coaching and development of employees. Millennial and Gen Z workers tend to value this kind of investment, but it's also critical to growing talented employees who have the right capabilities, but not necessarily the experience. This effort also reinforces inclusion by providing real sponsorship of employees with diverse backgrounds. For example, HubSpot moved from annual performance reviews to social performance management. It allows employees to receive continuous and instantaneous feedback from nearly anyone in the organization, encouraging ongoing skill development.

Earning a reputation for excellence across all these areas won't happen overnight. But the payoff is a high-caliber, diverse workforce hungry to help the company succeed in the new tech-enabled economy.

TAKEAWAYS

The demand for tech talent is extraordinarily high, with legacy companies and tech giants wooing the same limited number of workers. To fill these roles at a time when skilled people have many opportunities, consider what capabilities are truly essential (and which are trainable), and cultivate three factors to make your company a place where talented candidates want to work:

- ✓ **A commitment to diversity and inclusion.** Opening up more opportunities for underrepresented candidates is the right thing to do, helps retention, and widens your company's talent funnel.

- ✓ **Transparent and accountable senior management.** Managers should be visible and willing to engage directly with employees. The best talent will prefer a firm where they feel their work has real impact.

- ✓ **A culture of coaching and development.** These elements are critical to growing talented employees who have the right capabilities but not necessarily the experience.

Adapted from content posted on hbr.org, November 3, 2021 (product #H06OFH).

Section 2

FRESH TAKES ON MATURE TECH

WHAT LEADERS NEED TO KNOW ABOUT THE CLOUD

by Bhaskar Ghosh and Karthik Narain

Medical researchers and innovators are the heroes who are making our world livable again, but they can't do it without the power of technology—especially cloud computing. This critical technology enabled the rapid development of Covid-19 vaccines. Moderna, a relatively small organization compared to pharmaceutical giants, built and scaled its operations on the cloud, and was able to deliver its first clinical batch to the National Institutes of Health for phase one trial only 42 days after initial sequencing of the virus. To accomplish this, the company invented proprietary cloud-based technologies and methods to create mRNA constructs that cells recognize as if they were produced in the body. This allowed Moderna to experiment rapidly and easily shift between vaccines for different viruses without investing in new technology or infrastructure.

Moderna also uses the cloud to achieve higher efficiency and visibility across manufacturing, inventory management, and even accounting—and to "copy and paste" its digital manufacturing model onto partner facilities, which is critical for the rapid scaling of vaccine production.

The Moderna example reveals the cloud's connection to five key areas all CEOs must lead: speed to market, reduced costs, flexibility of operations, business resilience, and innovation capabilities. Cloud technology allows startups and midsize companies to access big tech capabilities—computing power, algorithms, programming tools, and architectures—and partner in an ecosystem with larger firms.

But prior to 2020, progress toward the cloud had actually been quite gradual. As we found in designing the research for our survey of 750 C-level leaders, about 20% to 30%

The authors thank Dave Light and H. James Wilson of Accenture Research for their contributions to this article.

of work is being done through the cloud, and companies initially planned to accelerate that to more like 80% over an 8- to 10-year process.[1] The pandemic, however, sped things up. Companies of all kinds quickly learned that they had to depend on cloud technologies to enable their entire staffs to work from home, to ramp up digital commerce, and to provide telehealth, entertainment streaming, and more. We now see this shift to 80% taking place in the near future.

Through our work with companies across the world, which includes dozens of in-depth discussions with C-level leadership, we identified the five key questions business leaders have as they strategize for the long term and move closer to that 80% target. Two are long-standing concerns about security and legacy IT. The other three ultimately come down to how the cloud makes it possible to help CEOs reimagine their business. If you're a business leader daunted by cloud adoption, consider our research- and experience-informed answers to these questions.

Can I Really Trust My Data in the Cloud?

There are two important points here. First, cloud providers operate comprehensive data security programs so you don't have to. On-premises infrastructure is prone to the kind of small mistakes that determined cyberattackers can exploit. The main public cloud providers, however, are able to provide advanced data security controls, including data encryption, database monitoring, and access control.

That said, security continues to be a legitimate concern, and companies would rightly (and often for legal reasons) refrain, for example, from putting sensitive consumer or health-care data in the public cloud. Most companies are addressing the desire to work through the cloud without exposing certain data to risk of exposure by turning to a hybrid model of public and private cloud operations. The latter allows businesses to maintain control over their most sensitive information.

Do I Have to Get Rid of My Legacy Infrastructure Once and for All?

Unwinding the spaghetti is difficult. And beyond the technical issues, the question of who pays for it can slow things down. Executives naturally aren't keen to start over from scratch; in fact, in a 2018 survey, 70% of C-level leaders told us they wanted to keep running legacy systems as long as possible despite the limits they set on innovation and market agility.[2]

What to do? A "lift-and-shift" strategy is a good approach for many companies. Imagine moving your entire house from one city to another without bothering to pack and unpack all the individual items or even rethink the layout of your rooms. For companies, this makes sense, because it causes minimal disruption to customers and provides relief from pressing concerns like outages. The rest can be worked out later.

How Do I Make the Right Cloud Choices for My Business?

The most important step here is to understand the three major cloud capabilities and what they make possible. Software as a service (SaaS) started the cloud revolution. Companies could roll it out quickly, fund it directly from business budgets, and standardize processes while also enabling innovation. As cloud computing matured, infrastructure as a service (IaaS) and platform as a service (PaaS) models emerged, giving businesses a higher level of control over the alignment of business and IT objectives.

The key for organizations is to understand the capabilities and strengths of each model and apply them judiciously to enable business innovation and growth. Here are a few simple rules of thumb: IaaS is a simple way to access computing and data storage resources. With IaaS, an organization rents servers and storage in the cloud rather than purchasing and maintaining its own infrastructure. PaaS is a popular choice for businesses that want to create unique applications without making major financial investments. And SaaS, the most commonly used cloud application service, is an important means for organizations to access software applications.

How Does Shifting Our Work to the Cloud Make It Possible to Reimagine the Business?

The cloud dissolves many of the limits on innovation. For example, in the pharmaceuticals industry, Takeda (an Accenture client) is using "edge" technology to help hemophiliacs monitor their enzymes while at home. (Edge computing, part of a cloud approach, is the ability to sense and respond to data locally, reducing latency and demands on communications technology.)

Also consider one of the issues at the top of mind for many CEOs today: sustainability.

French energy company ENGIE (also an Accenture client) is using the cloud to reinvent itself as a provider of renewable and low- or zero-carbon energy. The big challenge at the core of this radical business model change is understanding client preferences in 70 countries and making those insights accessible in all 24 of ENGIE's business units. Using a PaaS tool, the company created a single, unified view of each customer. ENGIE's marketing, sales, and service teams can now work together without silos and quickly deliver tailor-made solutions for its customers. Consider one example: ENGIE is working with the University of Iowa on a 50-year contract to help the school meet its energy, water, and sustainability goals on its two campuses in Iowa City. One goal is to make the school coal-free by 2025.

It's not just companies that benefit from cloud reinvention. The city of Barcelona has worked on a smart-city strategy culminating in a move to the cloud since 2013. The strategy enables the central management of urban transportation, traffic, waste disposal, noise, water, and energy on a single platform through internet of things sensors. This open-source platform also connects to other smart cities around the globe.

Business leaders understand the potential of the cloud in this area. In our survey, 87% said that the cloud would be a critical component, to a moderate or great degree, in achieving sustainability goals.

Do I Have the Skills I Need to Take Advantage of the Cloud?

When it comes to accelerating cloud initiatives, what's keeping CEOs up at night the most is probably a lack of skills in the organization. For companies that have been low adopters (those doing less than 30% of their work in the cloud), almost half of CEOs cited a lack of the needed skills as a barrier to success. But even for high adopters (companies doing 75% or more of their work in the cloud), three in 10 CEOs are concerned about skills shortages.

There's no shortcut here, but making aggressive plans is an essential first step. For example, Takeda's cloud-driven business transformation has big goals for innovation and how its people work. The company anticipates creating hundreds of new jobs in specialized roles, turning to new talent pools, and building the skills of thousands of employees so they can accelerate Takeda's data and digital capabilities. A lower-investment approach could be to encourage your people to seek out online instruction to build their skills. Make sure to give them time for this work and the assurance that you'll recognize the credentials.

Above all, it's vital for the CEO to become intimately involved in the cloud journey. The cloud is too important to a business's fundamental competitiveness to be treated as an IT program. It's about creating a platform for the efficiency, innovation, and growth that will determine the future success of your business.

For companies of all kinds, the pandemic accelerated a shift to the cloud to enable their staff to work from home, ramp up their digital commerce, and more. Leaders are enthusiastic about what the cloud can do, but they still have questions that require answers that are informed by research and experience.

- ✓ Public cloud providers have advanced security, but many companies should refrain from putting their most sensitive information in the cloud.

- ✓ There are strategies (such as "lift-and-shift") that can maintain legacy systems while taking advantage of the cloud.

- ✓ The cloud revolution began with a software-as-a-service model, but now infrastructure-as-a-service

and platform-as-a-service models are gaining
traction.

✓ The cloud can help you reimagine your business,
dissolve limits to innovation, and make progress
on your sustainability goals.

✓ If your company lacks the skills needed to take
advantage of the cloud, you can plan for the future
by immediately developing your employees' cloud
capabilities.

NOTES

1. Accenture, "Navigating the Barriers to Maximizing Cloud Value,"
https://www.accenture.com/_acnmedia/PDF-139/Accenture-Cloud
-Outcomes-Exec-Summary.pdf#zoom=40.

2. Accenture, "In the Blink of an I.T.," https://www.accenture.com/
_acnmedia/PDF-72/Accenture-Exponential-IT-Anthem.pdf#zoom
=50.

*Adapted from "What CEOs Need to Know About the Cloud in 2021" on hbr.org,
March 10, 2021 (product #H067SH).*

7

SAY GOODBYE TO COOKIES

by Tim Glomb

For years, companies have been using cookies—small text files stored on the browser that keep track of website visits—to monitor consumers' online behavior. Cookies can provide rich data that helps brands get a better sense of who their customers are and enables them to target those customers with more relevant offerings. But this personalization comes at a cost: Consumers are increasingly concerned about who is collecting this data, how much of their behavior is being tracked, what companies are doing with that information, and who they may be selling it to.

A Pew report found that 79% of Americans are concerned about the way companies use their data.[1] Forty-one percent of U.S. consumers regularly delete cookies, and 30% have installed an ad blocker.[2] And of course, this growing distrust has increasingly been reflected in government regulation. One of the most well-known pieces of legislation targeting cookies was the 2018 General Data Protection Regulation (GDPR), which substantially expanded data privacy requirements in the EU. More recently, European regulators have begun to call for a complete ban on ad targeting, both the states of Virginia and California have passed comprehensive privacy bills, and Google Chrome announced plans to end its support of third-party cookies altogether.

The era of cookies is coming to an end. But that doesn't mean that companies should abandon personalization; it's just time for a new, better approach.

The Rise of Zero-Party Data

So, what does it take to leverage the benefits of data-driven targeting without falling prey to the privacy issues (and mounting regulatory obstacles) that surround cookies? The answer lies in a concept known as *zero-party data*. In contrast to third-party data, which is passively collected from cookies and used by companies to make inferences about broad demographic segments of people, zero-party data refers to information that is intentionally and proactively shared directly by individual consumers.

Specifically, many brands have begun using mechanisms such as polls, quizzes, sweepstakes questionnaires, or interactive social media stories to collect explicitly opt-in data that provides highly specific insights into consumer preferences. This type of data collection is a win-win: It offers customers greater control and transparency into exactly what data is being collected, while giving companies access to more useful information that enables them to target personalized offers much more effectively.

When setting up these systems, it's important to remember that the problem with cookies isn't personalization— it's a lack of respect for consumer privacy, and an approach to personalization that often doesn't actually deliver useful information to the customer or the company. Consumers are increasingly interested in personalized offers, and zero-party data makes it possible to offer much better personalization than cookies ever could (without the privacy issues). In fact, a survey of more than 5,000 global respondents found a 33% year-over-year increase between 2020 and 2021 in the number of consumers interested in personalized offers.[3]

Customers are happy to receive ads and product offers that have been effectively matched to their needs—they just don't want their data to be collected in an opaque, insecure manner and then sold to the highest bidder. Zero-party data puts customers in control of what information they share and who they share it with, enabling both greater transparency and more effective personalization.

For example, as VP of content and data for enterprise marketing platform Cheetah Digital, I worked with one company that pivoted from traditional targeted ads to zero-party data strategy in early 2018. Over the course of three years, this company conducted more than 300 sweepstakes initiatives, reaching 750,000 unique entrants and gathering over 15 million data points. Consumers voluntarily provided information around which products they wanted to purchase, their budget for those products, which channels they'd prefer to purchase those products on, and when they'd like to purchase them, and the company then leveraged that detailed data set to develop dynamic, hyper-personalized email and SMS campaigns.

Those campaigns achieved open rates above 50% and click-to-buy rates nearing 20%, representing increases of 250% and 33%, respectively, compared to prior cookies-based campaigns. The company also used this data to define more than 50 incredibly granular audience segments for its ad campaigns, which resulted in engagement rates that were on average 5.7 times higher than campaigns using Google and Facebook's interest-targeting tools (tools which primarily leverage data from cookies).

The Future of Customer Engagement

Zero-party data is here—and it's only becoming more prevalent. Cookies are on their way out, and marketers who want to stay relevant are increasingly investing in a zero-party data approach. I've worked with countless companies both large and small that are making the leap, reenvisioning their marketing campaigns to leverage detailed data that customers freely provide rather than relying on cookies-driven targeting.

This may seem like a small technical shift, but it represents a fundamental philosophical change in how businesses think about their customers' data. While cookies operate in the background, passively collecting information to be used in often unclear, unscrupulous ways, zero-party data enables both greater personalization and greater control for the end user. Ultimately, zero-party data isn't just a new way to do targeted ads or email campaigns—it's about transforming how companies engage with (and demonstrate respect for) their most valuable stakeholders: their customers.

TAKEAWAYS

Cookies have long enabled companies to track their customers' web activity and use that data to personalize ads and product offerings, but they also pose serious privacy issues. Regulators, governments, and tech leaders are starting to crack down, so many companies are taking a new approach to collecting and leveraging customer information: zero-party data.

✓ Unlike third-party data, which is passively collected by cookies, zero-party data refers to information that consumers proactively share through mechanisms like polls, sweepstakes, and interactive social media stories.

✓ Zero-party data allows consumers to retain control over and visibility into their information.

✓ This new approach allows companies to offer far more effective personalization, transforming how they engage with their customers.

NOTES

1. Brooke Auxier et al., "Americans and Privacy: Concerned, Confused and Feeling Lack of Control Over Their Personal Information," Pew Research Center, November 15, 2019, https://www.pewresearch.org/internet/2019/11/15/americans-and-privacy-concerned-confused-and-feeling-lack-of-control-over-their-personal-information/.

2. Stefan Tornquist and Richard Jones, "Is Your Marketing Strategy Out of Touch?," Cheetah Digital, March 31, 2020, https://www.cheetahdigital.com/sites/default/files/2020-04/CheetahDigital_Econsultancy%20Report_%20Downloadable_%20All%20Data_Eng_04-01-20-FINAL.pdf.

3. Cheetah Digital, "Digital Consumer Trends Index 2021," https://www.cheetahdigital.com/sites/default/files/2021-03/Digital_Consumer_Trends_Index_2021.pdf.

Adapted from content posted on hbr.org, April 8, 2021 (product #H06AHH).

8

COULD RANSOMWARE ATTACKS ULTIMATELY BENEFIT CONSUMERS?

by Rahul Telang

I n early 2017, a data breach at the credit reporting agency Equifax resulted in the exposure of the private records of more than 40% of the American public. The breach occurred after Equifax neglected to patch a known vulnerability in its system, which allowed hackers to access Social Security numbers, driver's licenses, addresses, dates of birth, financial records, and more. Equifax eventually reached a settlement with the United States Federal Trade Commission in 2019, but—as is so often the case with big data breaches—the settlement inflicted little real pain on the company. Individual consumers, meanwhile, paid a big price for the company's inadequate security: Their personal information was irreversibly exposed and disseminated.

In economics, this kind of situation is known as externality, wherein an action by one party hurts another party, but that second party has no recourse. Regulators have often attempted to address this externality and lessen the burden it places on consumers, but they've had only limited success, largely because companies have seemed happy to settle cases after the fact if that means they don't have to make significant up-front investments in improved security.

But meaningful changes are likely to come soon, and in ways that will benefit consumers in the long term. That's because the leaders of companies that store valuable private information are being forced to defend their companies against the growing threat of ransomware attacks.

Ransomware attacks—launched by hackers who use malicious software to seize and block access to company computer systems until substantial money is paid for their release—have been in the news a lot lately. In the year prior to writing, ransomware attackers collected nearly $350 million from such companies as Kaseysa, the

Colonial Pipeline, Microsoft Exchange, and JBS USA, a figure that represented a threefold increase over the two previous years.

What explains the increase? Some important factors include the increased use of remote networks and systems during the Covid-19 lockdown, and growth in the cryptocurrency sphere, which has made it easier for hackers to extract ransoms.

That said, it's worth noting that ransomware attacks are no different from the typical security attacks that we've been reading about for years. There's nothing novel about the technology they rely on. What is novel, though, is that they're attacking companies rather than consumers, and that's changing the economics of data security.

In a traditional data breach, such as the one suffered by Equifax, companies only suffer indirectly from the harms caused by their inadequate attention to security. That surely explains why, according to data from Experian, 35% of companies have not updated their security plans since they were first put in place. IBM has estimated that the average cost of a data breach in the United States is $8.64 million, a cost that is often hard for companies to recognize or account for. A breach may lead to a tarnished reputation and cause a company to lose some business, but those problems tend to be temporary—and the overall cost of such a breach will almost surely be too diffuse for management to make it a key area of focus. Ultimately, it's a company's customers who suffer the most from a traditional breach because they're the ones whose information gets exposed.

Ransomware attacks have changed the nature of the game by attacking companies rather than consumers. This change, which forces companies to pay a steep and direct price for lax security, means that managers at all sorts of companies are going to have to focus in a newly serious way on improving cybersecurity and protecting their networks.

If you're a senior leader at a company that collects and uses customer data, here are a few basic steps you should take to make sure your company is protected against both ransomware attacks and traditional data breaches. Some of these steps are simple and inexpensive, and others are more involved and expensive. But they're all the right thing to do, and they'll benefit not only you, but also your customers.

Provide continuous training and reminders to employees about the threat of phishing attacks. Phishing has been around for a long time, of course, but it's no longer primarily just a nuisance. Attackers are getting serious, and lot of money is now at stake. Firms have to ensure that their employees understand the dangers and know how to recognize the warning signs. In-house phishing simulations—in which IT sends realistic-looking phishing emails to employees and then monitors their responses—can be very helpful, because they train employees to be vigilant, help IT understand system vulnerabilities, and allow firms to think in a targeted way about improving their cybersecurity.

Allow employees only to download apps and software and use programs that are required for work. Employees often don't like this because it's so convenient to be able to use work devices for personal purposes, but firms and IT departments need to tighten up their controls on this front. Most have been too lax about this for years. It's also important for managers to take the time to explain the need for this policy to everybody. Many third-party tools are available that can be installed on company computers and allow administrators to control which applications employees can install.

Make it a priority to patch vulnerabilities and keep systems up-to-date. Hackers can only execute ransomware attacks if they can get in your network. So make that as hard as possible by applying patches as quickly and as effectively as you can and by updating systems as soon as new versions become available. Patch management has always been part of IT services, but in the face of new dangers, firms need to make it a higher priority.

Back up your firm's data. If potential attackers know you have the ability to recover your information, then you become a much less promising target for a ransomware attack. Even if you can't back up all of your data, you can reduce the chance of attack by signaling that you have much of your information backed up. This can be an expensive and time-consuming job. CIOs have to carefully evaluate what data to back up, how frequently, what type of media to use for backup, and the cost to restore it if and when a ransomware attack takes place.

.   .   .

None of these practices is new, but many firms—assuming that the costs outweigh the benefits—have yet to adopt them. But with the threat of costly ransomware attacks rising rapidly, the time to get serious has arrived.

TAKEAWAYS

Ransomware attackers collect staggering sums from the companies they've attacked, hurting companies more directly than traditional data breaches; this means organizations may finally get more serious about cybersecurity. Here are necessary steps to take:

- ✓ **Provide continuous training and reminders to employees about the threat of phishing attacks.** Firms have to ensure that their employees understand the dangers and know how to recognize the warning signs.

- ✓ **Allow employees only to download apps and software and use programs that are required for work.** Many third-party tools are available that can be installed on company computers and allow administrators to control which applications employees can install.

- ✓ **Make it a priority to patch vulnerabilities and keep systems up-to-date.** In the face of new dangers, firms need to make patch management a higher priority.

- ✓ **Back up your firm's data.** If potential attackers know you have the ability to recover your information, then you become a much less promising target for a ransomware attack.

Adapted from content posted on hbr.org, August 2, 2021 (product #H06HW6).

Section 3

AI FOR THE REST OF US

9

AI DOESN'T HAVE TO BE TOO EXPENSIVE OR COMPLICATED

by Andrew Ng

Despite the vast potential of artificial intelligence (AI), it hasn't caught hold in most industries. Sure, it has transformed consumer internet companies such as Google, Baidu, and Amazon—all massive and data rich with hundreds of millions of users. But for projections that AI will create $13 trillion of value a year to come true, industries such as manufacturing, agriculture, and health care still need to find ways to make this technology work for them.[1] Here's the problem: The playbook that these consumer internet companies use to build their AI systems—where a single one-size-fits-all AI system can serve massive numbers of users—won't work for these other industries.

Instead, legacy industries will need a large number of bespoke solutions that are adapted to their many diverse uses. This doesn't mean that AI won't work for these industries, however. It just means they need to take a different approach.

To bridge this gap and unleash AI's full potential, executives in all industries should adopt a new, data-centric approach to building AI. Specifically, they should aim to build AI systems with careful attention to ensuring that the data clearly conveys what they need the AI to learn. This requires focusing on data that covers important cases and is consistently labeled, so that the AI can learn from this data what it is supposed to do. In other words, the key to creating valuable AI systems is that we need teams that can program with data rather than program with code.

Why Adopting AI Outside of Tech Can Be So Hard

Why isn't AI widely used outside consumer internet companies? The top challenges facing AI adoption in other industries include:

1. **Small data sets.** In a consumer internet company with huge numbers of users, engineers have millions of data points that their AI can learn from. But in other industries, the data set sizes are much smaller. For example, can you build an AI system that learns to detect a defective automotive component after seeing only 50 examples? Or to detect a rare disease after learning from just 100 diagnoses? Techniques built for 50 million data points don't work when you have only 50 data points.

2. **Cost of customization.** Consumer internet companies employ dozens or hundreds of skilled engineers to build and maintain monolithic AI systems that create tremendous value—say, an online ad system that generates more than $1 billion in revenue per year. But in other industries, there are numerous $1–$5 million projects, each of which needs a custom AI system. For example, each factory manufacturing a different type of product might require a custom inspection system, and every hospital, with its own way of coding health records, might need its own AI to process its patient data. The aggregate value of these hundreds of thousands of projects is massive, but the economics of an individual project might not support hiring a large,

dedicated AI team to build and maintain it. This problem is exacerbated by the ongoing shortage of AI talent, which further drives up the costs.

3. **Gap between proof of concept and production.** Even when an AI system works in the lab, a massive amount of engineering is needed to deploy it in production. It is not unusual for teams to celebrate a successful proof of concept, only to realize that they still have another 12–24 months of work before the system can be deployed and maintained.

For AI to realize its full potential, we need a systematic approach to solving these problems across all industries. The data-centric approach to AI, supported by tools designed for building, deploying, and maintaining AI applications—called machine learning operations (MLOps) platforms—will make this possible. Companies that adopt this approach faster will have a leg up relative to competitors.

Data-Centric AI Development

AI systems are made up of software—the computer program that includes an AI model—and data, the information used to train the model. For example, to build an AI system for automated inspection in manufacturing, an AI engineer might create software that implements a deep learning algorithm, which is then shown a data set comprising pictures of good and defective parts so it can learn to distinguish between them.

Over the last decade, a lot of AI research was driven by software-centric development (also called model-centric development) in which the data is fixed, and teams attempt to optimize or invent new programs to learn well from the available data. Many tech companies had large data sets from millions of consumers, and they used it to drive a lot of innovation in AI.

But at AI's current level of sophistication, the bottleneck for many applications is getting the right data to feed to the software. We've heard about the benefits of *big data*, but we now know that for many applications, it is more fruitful to focus on making sure we have *good data*— data that clearly illustrates the concepts we need the AI to learn. This means, for example, the data should be reasonably comprehensive in its coverage of important cases and labeled consistently. Data is food for AI, and modern AI systems need not only calories, but also high-quality nutrition.

Shifting your focus from software to data offers an important advantage: It relies on the people you already have on staff. In a time of great AI talent shortage, a data-centric approach allows many subject-matter experts who have vast knowledge of their respective industries to contribute to the AI system development.

For example, most factories have workers that are highly skilled at defining and identifying what counts as a defect (Is a 0.2 mm scratch a defect? Or is it so small that it doesn't matter?). If we expect each factory to ask its workers to invent new AI software as a way to get that factory the bespoke solution it needs, progress will be slow. But if we instead build and provide tools to empower these domain experts to engineer the data—by allowing them to express their knowledge about manufacturing through providing data to the AI—their odds of success will be much higher.

Make Building and Using AI Systematic and Repeatable

The shift toward data-centric AI development is being enabled by the emerging field of MLOps, which provides tools that make building, deploying, and maintaining AI systems easier than ever before. Tools that are geared to help produce high-quality data sets, in particular, hold the key to addressing the challenges of small data sets, the high cost of customization, and the long road to getting an AI project into production outlined earlier.

How, exactly? First, ensuring high-quality data means that AI systems will be able to learn from the smaller data sets available in most industries. Second, by making it possible for a business's domain experts, rather than AI experts, to engineer the data, the ability to use AI will become more accessible to all industries. And third, MLOps platforms provide much of the scaffolding software needed to take an AI system to production, so teams no longer have to develop this software. This allows teams to deploy AI systems and bridge the gap between proof of concept and production in weeks or months rather than years.

The vast majority of valuable AI projects have yet to be imagined. And even for projects that teams are already working on, the gap that leads to deployment in production remains to be bridged; indeed, Accenture estimates that 80% to 85% of companies' AI projects are in the proof-of-concept stage.[2]

Here are some things companies can do right now:

1. Instead of merely focusing on the *quantity* of data you collect, also consider the *quality*; make sure it clearly illustrates the concepts you need the AI to learn.

2. Make sure your team considers taking a data-centric approach rather than a software-centric

approach. Many AI engineers, including many with strong academic or research backgrounds, were trained to take a software-centric approach; urge them to adopt data-centric techniques as well.

3. For any AI project that you intend to take to production, be sure to plan the deployment process and provide MLOps tools to support it. For example, even while building a proof-of-concept system, urge the teams to begin developing a longer-term plan for data management, deployment, and AI system monitoring and maintenance.

It's possible for AI to become a thriving asset outside of data-rich consumer internet businesses, but it has yet to hit its stride in other industries. But because of this, the greatest untapped opportunity for AI may lie in taking it to these other industries. Just as electricity has transformed every industry, AI is on a path to do so, too. But the next few steps on that path will require a shift in our playbook for how we build and deploy AI systems. Specifically, a new data-centric mindset, coupled with MLOps tools that allow industry domain experts to participate in the creation, deployment, and maintenance of AI systems, will ensure that all industries can reap the rewards that AI can offer.

TAKEAWAYS

The software-centric approach to building AI used by tech giants doesn't translate for companies that don't have overflowing troves of data they can use to train models. Companies in industries such as agriculture, manufacturing, and health care need data-centric AI solutions that are adapted to their own diverse uses.

✓ These organizations should shift their focus from building the right model—a software-focused approach—to focusing on getting *good data*.

✓ New machine learning operations (MLOps) tools help produce high-quality data sets without high costs or long production times.

✓ For any AI project that you intend to take to production, be sure to employ the right MLOps tools to support it.

NOTES

1. Jacques Bughin et al., "Notes from the AI Frontier: Modeling the Impact of AI on the World Economy," McKinsey Global

Institute paper, https://www.mckinsey.com/~/media/McKinsey
/Featured%20Insights/Artificial%20Intelligence/Notes%20
from%20the%20frontier%20Modeling%20the%20impact%20
of%20AI%20on%20the%20world%20economy/MGI-Notes
-from-the-AI-frontier-Modeling-the-impact-of-AI-on-the-world
-economy-September-2018.ashx.

2. Accenture, "AI: Built to Scale," November 14, 2019, https://
www.accenture.com/us-en/insights/artificial-intelligence/ai
-investments.

Adapted from content posted on hbr.org, July 29, 2021 (product #H06HSP).

10

NO-CODE PLATFORMS CAN BRING AI TO SMALL AND MIDSIZE BUSINESSES

by Jonathon Reilly

Technology often follows a familiar progression. First, it's used by a small core of scientists; then the user base expands to engineers who can navigate technical nuance and jargon until finally it's made user-friendly enough that almost anyone can use it.

Right now, the process for building software is making that final leap. Just as the clickable icons of Windows and Mac OS replaced obscure DOS commands, new "no-code" platforms are replacing programming languages with simple drag-and-drop interfaces. The implications are huge: Where a team of engineers was once required to build a piece of software, now users with a web browser and an idea have the power to bring that idea to life themselves. This means that powerful tech, which only large, well-resourced businesses have been able to afford, is suddenly within the reach of even small companies.

Perhaps most significantly, it's making it possible to deploy AI without hiring an army of expensive developers and data scientists. That means that smaller businesses, which often have huge amounts of data, can employ the benefits of AI such as powering new kinds of customer experiences (like a self-driving Tesla), growing companies' top line (like P&G's AI-driven advertising spend), and optimizing operations for maximum efficiency (like Walmart's supply chain).

For smaller businesses, knowing where and how to deploy this tech can be daunting. Like larger companies, which may have already gone through the process of figuring out how data science might work for them, it makes sense to begin by deploying no-code AI on bite-size tasks versus ocean-boiling megaprojects. Ideally, you want to:

- Work with the data you already have. There is often more value to be captured there than you may initially think.

- Pick high-value tasks where being more efficient will drive growth.

- Get quick wins in common areas, sales funnel optimization, or churn reduction, so your team can learn how AI applies to a wide range of use cases.

- Don't be afraid to move on quickly if you cannot achieve a 10x ROI from any AI project. There are plenty of high-return applications where you can get value.

No-code tools empower employees to think creatively about using data to drive or optimize their work—and consequently, the business.

Consider an example like intelligent lead scoring. Sales teams collect leads from all kinds of places—web scraping, cold calling, online forms, business cards dropped in a bowl at a trade show. But once a team has thousands of leads, the problem is deciding which ones to chase down.

By spotting patterns in user behavior, demographics, and firmographics, a simple no-code classification model, for example, can rank leads according to their probability of turning into sales—a task where many large firms use AI.

Using a no-code AI platform, a user can drag and drop a spreadsheet of data about sales prospects into the interface, make a few selections from a drop-down menu, and click a couple of buttons. The platforms will build a model and return a spreadsheet with leads sorted, from the hottest to the coldest, enabling salespeople to maximize revenue by focusing on the prospects that are most likely to buy.

The advantage of no-code platforms is that they are not restricted to any particular use case. These tools can detect machine maintenance patterns and predict which machines need attention before they fail or be used by marketing teams to spot dissatisfaction and reduce churn or by operations teams to reduce employee attrition. They can spot patterns in text, not just numbers, and analyze sales notes and transcripts alongside sales history and marketing data, allowing companies to automate complex processes.

For many companies, working with no-code platforms will come down to simply finding the right project—and the right platform.

Where to Start with No-Code

A competent no-code platform needs three critical features.

First, it needs a simple interface that makes it easy to get data into the model training process. That means integrating with today's popular business systems, such as customer relationship management systems like Salesforce, and spreadsheet software, such as Excel. If relevant data lives in multiple places, the platform should be able to merge it.

Once the data is uploaded, the platform needs to be able to automatically classify and correctly encode the data for the model training process—all with minimal input from the user. For example, the platform might identify columns in the data as categories, dates, or numbers, and the user should check to see that the columns are labeled correctly.

Second, the platform needs to automate model selection and training—tasks that data scientists would normally perform. There are many machine-learning approaches, and each works best on a specific type of problem. The platform should have a search mechanism to find the best model based on the data and the prediction required. The user should not need to know their way around regression or k-nearest neighbor algorithms. The platform should just deliver what works best.

Finally, the platform needs to be simple and easy to deploy with existing processes. It should be able to monitor model performance over time and retrain as the business environment shifts and new data becomes available.

How to Pick the Right No-Code Platform

Not all no-code AI platforms are made the same, and the right tool depends on a company's business needs. Solutions range from just a few dollars a month to enterprise platforms that cost six figures a year.

Finding the right one for a particular company may require some trial and error. The good news is that the best platforms are open, which means that anyone can try them to see how they work. In other words, users can take the platforms for test drives on relevant tasks.

For example, users can compare the accuracy of various platforms based on their relative performance on public data sets, such as the Australian credit approval data set where the goal is to classify credit card eligibility. With minimal effort, users can see how often each no-code AI platform is correct when it predicts an outcome in the validation set—a random selection of training data, typically

20%, that is held back and run against the model to measure performance.

But accuracy can sometimes be misleading. It's also important to consider the number of false positives and false negatives in prediction results. This is particularly valuable for "imbalanced" data sets, where only a small number of cases, like credit card fraud or cancer, need to be detected within large amounts of data.

For example, if a model to predict credit card fraud said "no fraud" every time, it would have very high accuracy, but would be useless. A good no-code platform will score false positives and false negatives.

Users should also consider the time it takes to use these no-code platforms. One key metric is the time for the platforms to train their models. That can vary from minutes to hours, and if it takes hours, it won't fit easily into a busy person's day.

Training is not the only time consideration. For these platforms to be truly transformative in an organization, they must be so simple to use that nontechnical people will adopt them into their workflow. Check the onboarding processes of various platforms. If they require help from the IT department or even significant effort, the people in sales or accounting aren't likely to bother.

For more companies to wield the power of AI in more applications across their business, the answer can't be "create and hire more data scientists." As little as a quarter of 1% of the world knows how to code. There's no doubt that no-code is the future.

Someday every part of every business will be AI optimized. The data is there today. The rate of progress and maturation of the platforms that let more and more people turn that data into AI-driven prediction and optimization machines will determine the speed at which it happens.

Removing friction from adoption will help unleash the power of AI across all industries and allow nonspecialists to literally predict the future. In time, no-code AI platforms will be as ubiquitous as word-processing or spreadsheet software is today.

TAKEAWAYS

New "no-code" platforms are replacing programming languages with simple drag-and-drop interfaces. Tech that was previously too labor-intensive and expensive for smaller companies, such as AI, is now increasingly within reach. But finding the right platform may require some trial and error. Companies should look for three things in a no-code platform:

- ✓ A simple interface that makes it easy to get data into the model training process

- ✓ Automated model selection and training (tasks that would normally be performed by data scientists)

- ✓ Simple and easily deployed with existing processes

Adapted from content posted on hbr.org, November 5, 2021 (product #H06OHE).

HOW WAREHOUSE WORKERS REALLY FEEL ABOUT AUTOMATION

by Joe Lui, Raghav Narsalay, Rushda Afzal, Ida Nair Sharma, and Dave Light

As of 2019, the global warehouse automation market—that is, programmable machines that pick, sort, and return goods to their shelves, as well as sensor- and AI-based tools that simplify tasks for warehouse workers—was worth about $15 billion. That number is expected to double by 2026, with supply chain leaders in an internal

Accenture survey citing warehouse automation as one of their top three priorities for digital investment. Clearly, the industry has huge growth potential. But what does this mean for the millions of workers currently employed in warehouses around the world?

In the United States alone, some 1.5 million workers are employed in the warehouse and storage sector. The UK's transportation and storage sector employs 1.8 million, and millions more work in warehouses worldwide. While some prior research has explored the impact of automation on these workers, there is still limited understanding of how automated technologies are changing their daily lives.[1] To get a better sense of workers' perspectives, we built on Accenture's research into warehouse automation with a series of in-depth video interviews with 34 warehouse workers and 33 frontline supervisors across the United States, UK, France, Spain, and China (interviews were conducted in workers' native languages, and then translated into English for analysis).[2]

We had three questions for workers:

1. How do automation technologies help you do your current job?

2. How do you feel about working side by side with a robot? What do you like and dislike about it?

3. What safety challenges are you facing in the warehouse?

And two questions for supervisors:

1. How has automation impacted operations and your role in the warehouse?

2. What are some of the new challenges that have emerged since deploying automation?

We then conducted a sentiment analysis and leveraged standard data science techniques to extract key themes from the responses. We found that overall, sentiment was about 40% negative and 60% positive, and we further identified a number of recurring concerns and hopes: On the negative side, workers were worried about losing their jobs, having inadequate training resources, and dealing with downtime or errors caused by technology malfunctions. On the positive side, workers expressed optimism that automation would make their jobs safer, increase productivity, and improve the quality of their work.

Workers have some concerns related to automation . . .

1. Fear of job loss. In our analysis, 42% of the responses categorized by our models as "negative sentiment" were related to fears around job loss. Two respondents from

China—Xin, a warehouse packer, and Chensi, a warehouse supervisor—used the exact same phrase to express their fears, saying, "This choice [to use robots] may cause us to face unemployment." Heather, a warehouse clerk at a global logistics company based in the UK, wondered about her future, commenting, "I don't mind working side by side to a robot, but I feel that sometimes my job is being pushed out to robots."

Even for those who weren't necessarily worried about their own jobs, many of the people we talked to expressed concern about others losing their livelihoods. As Sami, a French warehouse packer, explained: "It worries me for the following generations, because they will not need us anymore. . . . Everything will be done by robots, because [a machine] does not break its back, it is all automatic, it does not complain, and it does not strike." Similarly, UK-based supervisor Ramsay felt that "the negative thing is the fact that it removes jobs for people in this very difficult time."

2. Inadequate training. The next most common concern, accounting for 35% of all the negative responses, was a fear that inadequate training resources would reduce workers' ability to succeed in a new, digital workplace. Ricardo, a warehouse supervisor from Madrid, had mixed feelings about automation, explaining: "I think the more

the warehouse is automated, the better we'll all perform. Robots will greatly diminish our workloads, reduce risks, and increase productivity. But if we don't know how to handle them, they're hardly going to do any good." Similarly, a supervisor at a network technologies company in China, Kexin, noted that the demographic makeup of his workforce posed a challenge when it came to learning to use new tools: "Our current sorting technicians are older people," he noted. "It is a process of adjustment for them to learn to operate new smart equipment."

Workers in nonsupervisor roles expressed similar fears: Montserrat, a warehouse worker in Spain, shared that, for him, "the biggest challenge is understanding how this whole computer thing works and how to properly handle the robots and use the program commands." A packer for a U.S. sporting goods company expressed a similar sentiment, sharing: "I think I would feel a little uncomfortable at first working with robots just because it's new. . . . It would be a little nerve-racking at first, [but] once I have the proper training on how to interact with them and safety measures like shutdowns and things like that, I'd feel more confident and comfortable." Some workers also pointed out that while leaders might assume that most people have a certain level of familiarity with automated tools, that's not necessarily the case. As Axelle, a worker in a French warehouse, explained, "We need to learn how to use these robots correctly, to maneuver them, because we don't necessarily know anything more than how to drive a car."

3. Unreliable technology. Finally, the remaining concerns expressed in our interviews were related to fears that if automated tools broke down, workers would have no way to fix the problem, and would thus be unable to get their work done effectively. Especially when training resources are limited, workers may feel helpless when things go wrong, unable to address or even diagnose the issue. For instance, Eva, a supervisor at a global automotive manufacturer in Spain, described how "while working with the automated robots, we face challenges when a part is jammed or when they can't move. We learn about many codes only as the error happens." As Connor, a supervisor at a large UK-based retail company succinctly put it, when the system goes down and work has to be done manually, it's "an absolute pain."

Similarly, Dave, a material handler for a construction equipment manufacturer in the UK, felt that automated technologies have "definitely assisted," but when there are problems, "it generally ends up being a big breakdown," significantly disrupting his workday. When automated tools malfunction, workers are often forced to either take on additional manual labor or waste time waiting around for a technical expert to resolve the issue.

. . . But there is also cause for optimism

1. Greater safety. The number one factor driving workers' optimism around automation (mentioned in 42% of the positive responses) was its potential to improve safety. In many cases, safety referred to reducing wear and tear on the body: For example, Yanis, a forklift operator at a global logistics provider in France, told us, "I used to be on sick leave several times due to severe back pain. The automated forklift truck has improved the most important aspect of my physical health."

In addition, automated tools designed to sanitize workspaces became especially critical during the pandemic, preventing the spread of the coronavirus among workers whose jobs had to be done in person. Lanisha, a stocking associate at a retail chain in Michigan, stressed that her warehouse was safer because "with just the push of a button, the cleaning robots drive around cleaning the floors and wiping everything down the whole night."

2. Increased speed and efficiency. While executives often tout the high-level efficiency gains of automation, we were encouraged to see that on-the-ground workers and supervisors were similarly positive about the speed and efficiency made possible by implementing automated tools.

Thirty-eight percent of the positive responses fell into this category, with workers expressing their enthusiasm about technologies that helped them do their jobs faster and more efficiently.

Steve, a warehouse worker with a multinational food manufacturer in the UK, commented that "robots have made the warehouse massively more efficient." Alain, a materials handler at a French grocery wholesaler, noted that "we've gained something like ten times in terms of productivity," while Lilin, a packer at a casting equipment manufacturer in China, explained: "The robots easily lift several tons of cargo . . . [freeing up] people to do less strenuous tasks, like controlling the machines and inventory." Supervisors were similarly excited about the potential gains in efficiency: For example, UK-based warehouse supervisor Ian commented that "automated software makes it easier for me to do my job, as it's more efficient to use robots than to use humans [for some tasks]."

3. Higher-quality work. Finally, the remaining 20% of positive responses focused on how support from automated tools enabled workers to do their jobs better. One area in which we saw optimism that automation would improve the quality of work was in customer experience. A supervisor in a warehouse in China that had not yet invested in automation lamented that he received many customer complaints about "sorting errors and the shipment of expired foods." He expressed a hope that his company would invest in automated equipment soon, to prevent such complaints in the future. Similarly, Aryona, a Florida-based warehouse operator at a multinational consumer electronics retailer, described how automation reduced mistakes in the checkout process: "A lot of times there can be human error in the systems," she explained. "Having technologies that help to improve the quality is great."

In addition, many workers felt that automated tools not only helped them do a better job on discrete tasks, but also freed up their time for more interesting work, helping them stay motivated and engaged. For example, a supervisor in France, Thierry, expressed the difference automation made for him: "[Now,] I only intervene if there is a technical problem. It makes my role more interesting and less repetitive." For Andrew, a supervisor in the UK, automation meant he had "less supervision to carry out so [he could] focus on other tasks." Similarly, French warehouse worker Fabien appreciated how "working with robots makes the job more interesting. It saves you time, because you don't have to go looking for information. . . . Everything is already integrated and digested by the robots."

What Companies Should Do

Clearly, the automation of warehouse operations has the potential to make a real, positive impact on workers, but it's not without its downsides. Given the hopes and concerns our analyses revealed, we've identified a few strategies to help employers better support their workers while reaping the benefits of automation.

Emphasize growth opportunities

The number one fear expressed by the workers in our study was that automation might cost them their jobs. Of course, the flip side of that fear is the hope that automation could make workers' jobs safer and more meaningful. Both to address this fear and to emphasize its positive counterpart, employers must proactively expand growth opportunities (and make sure that workers have the tools and information they need to take advantage of those opportunities).

For example, some companies have launched training centers to help entry-level warehouse workers succeed in their current roles and provide paths for career growth. Importantly, these training programs aren't just about making resources available; they're about demonstrating that real growth is possible. That means not just encouraging employees to participate, but also ensuring that a substantial proportion of entry-level workers do in fact end up moving up the ranks into management positions, helping current workers envision how a similar trajectory could be within their reach.

Get the training right

Our interviews also highlighted workers' concerns around getting the training they need to work safely and fix issues with automated tools when they arise. Unfortunately, many well-intentioned employers struggle to provide training that actually works, especially for workers who start their jobs with little or no technical expertise in operating the kinds of robotic systems that are common in automated warehouses.

To get workers and supervisors comfortable with automated technologies, training programs must go beyond simple instructional videos or classroom sessions, and instead offer hands-on practice and simulations on how to operate these machines, as well as how to reset them when they malfunction. For example, FedEx uses VR simulations and gamified training programs to train its thousands of warehouse employees, allowing them to practice difficult tasks before they even set foot on the loading docks. These programs are designed to improve both worker safety and confidence, and they have substantially reduced turnover among package handlers.

Keep investing in safety

The biggest advantage of automation that the workers in our study identified was its capacity to boost safety. But while these new tools can enable a safer workplace, that doesn't mean that employers should stop investing in further improvements. Robotic assistants can save a good deal of wear and tear on the human body, but they don't solve everything. In many cases, human workers are still expected to do a lot of lifting or other strenuous tasks, and it's up to employers to provide as safe and healthy a workplace as possible.

One option is to pursue additional technological solutions. Some warehouses and manufacturing facilities have begun providing workers with exoskeletons for motion assistance, reducing the risk of physical injury or excessive fatigue. Newer robotic exoskeletons even use artificial intelligence to adjust to the individual wearing them, providing another level of support for workers. Companies have also begun using wearable sensors to capture workers' movement data, which they then use to assess injury risk on an individual level and provide feedback and training to improve safety. Similar tools were adapted during the pandemic to support social distancing by alerting workers when sensors indicated that they were too close together.

But even without advanced technologies, there's a lot employers can do to boost workers' health and safety. Simpler strategies can be similarly impactful, such as allocating sufficient cleaning staff to the warehouse floor to ensure a consistently sanitary workspace, providing clear signage around dangerous machinery, or instituting systems that encourage leadership to work proactively with on-the-ground workers to identify and address safety concerns.

TAKEAWAYS

Automated tools that help to lift, sort, and move goods around warehouses can substantially improve efficiency and quality. But how do the millions of workers employed in warehouses worldwide feel about these changes? A series of interviews with workers identified several common hopes and concerns as well as some possible solutions.

✓ The most frequently mentioned concerns were fear of job loss, lack of training for machines and systems, and unreliable technology.

✓ The workers were optimistic about automation bringing greater safety, more speed and efficiency, and higher-quality work.

✓ To address employees' fears and build on their hopes, leaders should emphasize and expand growth opportunities for entry-level workers, provide effective training to help workers learn to use automated tools, and invest in systems to ensure workers' health and safety.

NOTES

1. Lynda Gratton, "What Employees Tell Us About Automation and Re-skilling," *MIT Sloan Management Review*, December 18, 2019, https://sloanreview.mit.edu/article/what-employees-tell-us -about-automation-and-re-skilling/.

2. Accenture, "Value-Driven Warehouse Automation," https:// www.accenture.com/_acnmedia/PDF-156/Accenture-Value -Driven-Warehouse-Automation-Final.pdf.

Adapted from "Research: How Do Warehouse Workers Feel About Automation?" on hbr.org, February 11, 2022 (product #H06UY6).

Section 4

TRUST ME

DO YOUR DIGITAL DESIGN CHOICES TAKE ADVANTAGE OF CUSTOMERS?

by Michael Luca and Fiona Scott Morton

When tech companies exploit customers, they risk undermining trust in the entire digital ecosystem. One common form of exploitation occurs when digital platforms are designed to take advantage of customers' behavioral biases. Managers need to understand these biases and make a good faith effort to earn customer trust with ethical platform design choices.

Policy makers in Europe and the UK have studied how the design and architecture of online interactions impact consumers and markets, and they have already issued regulations to protect consumers. More recently, the U.S. Federal Trade Commission has begun to study the issue as well, but currently there are few constraints on firm behavior. When consumers are likely to be harmed, well-designed regulation can protect consumers as well as the firms that abide by the rules.

But companies must also play a proactive role in this process. There are concrete steps managers can take to support their consumers and to deliver more trust-worthy and customer-friendly technology. To see how customer exploitation has come to be so prevalent, and how to avoid engaging in it, it's helpful to understand the economics literature that has investigated one form of customer exploitation: the systematic exploitation of behavioral biases.

Twentieth-century economic analyses often assumed that people were unrealistically sophisticated in their day-to-day decisions—using all information available, unaffected by the way an issue is "framed," and virtually never making mistakes. Over the past several decades, a growing body of research has explored the ways in which decision-making systematically differs from this assumption. This work has documented a variety of systematic behavioral biases, such as the tendency to notice only the most salient information, to be influenced by small changes to the framing of choices, to stick with whatever default a company sets even if there are better options, and to overdiscount the future in favor of immediate benefit.

The Four Biases

Companies face an ethical and strategic choice when serving consumers with behavioral biases. They can try to debias their customers. They can work around—or accommodate—customer biases, while trying to act in the best interest of customers. Or, they can exploit behavioral biases for short-term profit. At the risk of stating the obvious, companies should work to avoid exploiting customers' biases. Here, we provide an overview of several biases that are commonly present in online contexts.

Bias 1: Customer inattention

Consumers cannot give their full attention and cognition to all pieces of information about every product and service they buy. Therefore, they react most strongly to the information that is more salient. Importantly, this saliency may be chosen and created by the firm itself. Research by Michael, in collaboration with Ginger Zhe Jin and Daniel Martin, suggests that customers do not fully account for the strategic component of such disclosure decisions— leading to costly mistakes and consumer harm.[1] Platforms often manipulate consumer attention, from the order in which search results are shown to the extent to which paid content is placed above organic content, among other techniques.

For example, StubHub shrouds fees on tickets, making it hard for customers to compute and compare the total costs they should expect to pay (which we examine in more detail later). Google uses much of its main search page to draw attention to paid ads and its own content, crowding out the organic search results that are potentially most useful to customers.

Bias 2: Reference dependence and framing effects

How product choices are framed, and which reference points are provided, can also impact how consumers make selections. For example, consider an example from Dan Ariely's 2008 book *Predictably Irrational*: A magazine offers three subscriptions—one for its digital content for $59, one for its print subscription for $125, and one for both its print and digital content for $125. Why would anyone buy only the print subscription when they can get print and digital for the same price? They wouldn't, and that's precisely the point. The middle option is likely present only to make the $125 print and digital option seem like a better deal—known as a decoy effect.

Decoy pricing is only one form of framing that can be exploitative. Consider the dire warnings often presented to customers to get them to purchase insurance: "Buy now before it's too late." "If you fail to protect your device, you will be responsible for all damage." "Seventy percent of people have protected their device. Will you?" These messages are often designed to leverage insights from behavioral economics to nudge customers to make a purchase, at times with little regard for whether the purchase is ultimately good for the customer.

Bias 3: Default bias

People tend to select the default option, even if better options are available, and even if the choice will have a major effect on their lives. As mentioned earlier, this can in principle be used in ways that will help people. For example, economists James Choi, David Laibson, Brigitte Madrian, and Andrew Metrick set out to understand the impact of defaults on 401(k) enrollment and found that changes as simple as setting the default to "enroll" versus "not enroll" significantly increases the chance of enrollment.[2] (They found similar results when they changed the default contribution rate as well.) But there are plenty of examples where auto-enrollment and strategic defaults can be set in ways that leave users worse off, so these decisions need to be made carefully.

Bias 4: Addiction and present bias

Research estimates that nearly a third of social media consumption is driven by addiction.[3] More broadly, digital addiction may lead people to stay online longer than they planned or wish to. This can be exacerbated by business models and the ways in which companies use algorithms and analytics. Tech companies regularly measure user engagement as an outcome and as a success metric. This can lead to outcomes where engagement increases but where customer well-being may suffer. As a user's outside options become more pressing (sleep, homework, loading the dishwasher), a platform might even use stronger measures to keep the user engaged.

Five Questions Your Brand Must Consider

By more carefully examining the risk of harm and the behavioral foundations of decision-making, managers can more proactively and ethically apply the use of algorithms and experimentation. This can help brands apply guardrails and invest in making sure to measure outcomes, so that they can avoid unwittingly exploiting behavioral biases.

When making design choices on a platform, managers should step back from short-term and narrow metrics like conversions and think through the broader questions about the value they create for their stakeholders. Here, we examine these questions and provide specific and actionable recommendations for managers.

1. Are you transparent about prices and fees?

In 2015, StubHub set out to brand itself as a transparent ticket seller. Marketing materials promised: "No surprise fees at checkout." When searching for tickets, users would see the prices, including all fees, up front to make it easier to search for tickets and know exactly what they'll pay. However, the transparent approach turned out to be short lived.

StubHub ran an experiment in which it compared its transparent system to a system in which it showed the base ticket price on the main search page and the full price only at checkout.[4] StubHub users who weren't shown fees until checkout spent about 21% more on tickets and were 14% more likely to complete a purchase compared with those who saw the total cost of a ticket up front. The company dropped its transparent approach and went back to shrouded fees.

While this may have been profitable in the short run, it comes with risks, including that customers will eventually tire of the lack of transparency and seek to purchase elsewhere and that new regulation will be imposed to limit how much a company can shroud its prices.

2. Do you make it easy to cancel your service?

Signing up for services online is typically easy, but canceling is often quite difficult. Firms create barriers and hassle by requiring consumers to take many steps to end the relationship. They use framing and persuasion to try to prevent cancellation: "Are you sure you want to cancel?" "You could pause instead." "Remember all the benefits of membership!"

Adding and subtracting services would likely be more symmetric in a more consumer-friendly market. For example, if the service can be bought online, a standard cancellation should not require the consumer to mail in a paper letter. If the service can be initiated with one click, it should generally be just as easy to cancel.

3. Do you use default settings in a way that is genuinely helpful for customers?

When you decide where to preset a default option for customers, ask yourself the following questions: Am I helping users make good decisions through this setting? Are my consumers actively choosing everything they pay for? Are defaults set so that no consumer must "opt out" to avoid purchasing?

Companies should research customer preferences to implement ethical defaults. If research shows that most people choose the second-highest price tier for a set of products or services, this might be a reasonable default choice. In general, the default should not be set to cause the consumer to purchase something that is optional and that they did not actively choose. This is called "opt-out" design, and it captures consumers who are not paying attention or make an error. Purchase expenditures should generally be opt in for consumers.

4. Do you frame choices in a misleading way?

To maintain long-term customer satisfaction, options should be presented in a way that allows customers to make decisions in their own best interest. When framing a decision, ask yourself: What decisions would the company's customers make if they were fully informed and had plenty of time to think through the decision?

Customers don't always buy a cheaper product if they spend more time considering their options. For example, when the Massachusetts Health Connector switched from showing all plan choices on one screen to requiring consumers to first choose a generosity level and next choose a branded plan, more consumers chose more generous (and expensive) plans, according to research by economists Keith Ericson and Amanda Starc published in the *Journal of Health Economics*.[5]

5. Do you create content that is addictive?

Managers should consider the habits they lead customers to form. Research has found, for instance, that teenagers who spend more time online and less time with friends tend to be less happy—suggesting that elements of online activity may be addictive. Among other corners of the tech sector, this is relevant in social media: A field experiment by economists Hunt Alcott, Luca Braghieri, Sarah Eichmeyer, and Matt Gentzkow seeks to understand the extent to which social media is addictive, experimentally varying the amount of time that people spend on social media by paying some people to stay off-line.[6] The team estimates that nearly a third of time spent on social media is a result of addiction. Digital addiction has important implications for managers, for consumer protection, and even for antitrust enforcement—as shown in research by Fiona, with psychiatrist James Niels Rosenquist and law professor Samuel Weinstein.[7]

Spending less time online can lead to increased happiness. But an ad-supported revenue model, such as YouTube's, changes the incentives of managers at every level to create addictive products that foster constant, uninterrupted engagement. YouTube's decision to automatically start a new video immediately after the previous one ends is an example of a brand choosing engagement that may be sacrificing the well-being of customers. If you dig around on YouTube support, it states, "If you're on YouTube on your computer, Autoplay is switched on by default." (It says the same is true for mobile web and the YouTube app.) In other words, YouTube requires you to opt out if you would prefer to watch one video at a time.

Companies should also think about how their business model impacts their incentives for creating an addictive product. Subscription models might create an incentive for the service to provide long-term value and engagement, with less incentive to keep users on the platform all day, every day.

Regulation Will Level the Digital Playing Field

We believe in the potential of the internet. But we also believe that the internet needs improved regulation. Like any powerful tool, it serves society best when it has appropriate safeguards. There is a reason we have created traffic lights and crash test standards and mandated driver's licenses, seatbelts, and airbags in automobiles. Automobiles are a powerful and useful form of transportation that delivers a much higher net benefit to society when regulated in these ways. Consumer protection plays the same role off-line, in areas like finance and food. However, it is vastly underdeployed online—an issue we discuss in a Yale Tobin Center for Economic Policy report as part of an ongoing digital regulation project.[8]

We believe digital consumer protection is necessary, and regulation will certainly play a major role in making digital commerce more trustworthy. But regulation isn't enough. Executives must play a proactive role in making sure their digital design functions in the best interests of customers. Doing so has the potential to give the company a deeper and more positive relationship with its customers, and to avoid the reputational risks associated with customer exploitation. And, importantly, when regulation arrives, the company will already be well positioned to abide by the new standards and to help create a more trustworthy internet.

TAKEAWAYS

Digital design that functions in the best interests of users has the potential to give companies a deeper and more positive relationship with their customers. Brands whose sites exploit consumer behavioral bias might benefit in the short term but can cause lasting harm to their reputation and the nature of trust on the internet. To assess how your digital design is influencing your customer relationships, consider the following questions:

✓ Are you being transparent in user agreements?

✓ Do you make canceling your services easy?

✓ Are your default options the best options for customers?

✓ Do you frame choices in a misleading way?

✓ Is your product addictive?

NOTES

1. Ginger Zhe Jin, Michael Luca, and Daniel Martin, "Is No News (Perceived as) Bad News? An Experimental Investigation of Information Disclosure," *American Economic Journal* 13, no. 2 (May 2021): 141–73; and Ginger Zhe Jin, Michael Luca, and Daniel Martin, "Complex Disclosure," HBS working paper no. 18–105, May 21, 2018, revised April 20, 2021, https://papers.ssrn.com/sol3/papers.cfm?abstract_id=3182586.

2. James J. Choi et al., "For Better or Worse: Default Effects and 401(k) Savings Behavior," in *Perspectives on the Economics of Aging,* ed. David A Wise (Chicago: University of Chicago Press, 2007), pp. 81–126.

3. Hunt Allcott et al., "The Welfare Effects of Social Media," *American Economic Review* 110, no. 3 (March 2020): 629–76.

4. Tom Blake et al., "Price Salience and Product Choice," *Marketing Science* 40, no. 4 (July 2021): 619–36.

5. Keith M. Marzilli Ericson and Amanda Starc, "How Product Standardization Affects Choice: Evidence from the Massachusetts Health Insurance Exchange," *Journal of Health Economics* 50 (2016): 71–85.

6. Allcott et al., "Welfare Effects of Social Media."

7. James Niels Rosenquist, Fiona M. Scott Morton, and Samuel N. Weinstein, "Addictive Technology and Its Implications for Antitrust Enforcement," *North Carolina Law Review* 100, no. 2 (2021): 432–82.

8. Gregory S. Crawford et al., "Digital Regulation Project: Consumer Protection for Online Markets and Large Digital Platforms," Yale Tobin Center for Economic Policy paper, May 20, 2021, https://tobin.yale.edu/sites/default/files/pdfs/digital%20regulation%20papers/Digital%20Regulation%20Project%20-%20Consumer%20Protection%20-%20Discussion%20Paper%20No%201.pdf.

Adapted from content posted on hbr.org, August 23, 2021 (product #H06JFK).

HOW DIGITAL TRUST VARIES AROUND THE WORLD

by Bhaskar Chakravorti, Ajay Bhalla, and Ravi Shankar Chaturvedi

T he pandemic forced rapid digitalization all around the world: Schools transformed to support online learning, many jobs became entirely remote, and automation accelerated in a wide array of industries. This digital growth demonstrated the tremendous capacity for technology to add value to our society, but it also revealed how fragile these tools—and people's trust in those tools—can be.

To build trust in the digital systems that connect us all, it is essential first to understand how people do (or don't) trust their digital ecosystems today. To that end, in partnership with Mastercard and Tufts University's Fletcher School, we conducted a large-scale analysis that explored global variation in four key components of digital trust: the security and trustworthiness of an economy's digital environment; the quality of the digital user experience; the extent to which users trust their digital environment; and the extent to which users actually use the digital tools available to them.

The resulting Digital Trust Scorecard (an updated and expanded edition of the framework we published in 2018) is accompanied by an interactive policy simulator and examines these four metrics of trust across 42 economies.[1] Next, we describe how we measured each of these four dimensions and then discuss some of the implications of our findings.

Environment, Experience, Attitudes, and Behavior

The first metric we considered was *digital environment*. This refers to the various mechanisms an economy has

The authors are grateful to Griffin Brewer, Christina Filipovic, and the Digital Planet team at the Fletcher School, and Paul Trueman at Mastercard.

in place to ensure safe and secure online ecosystems. These can include both public-sector institutions, such as regulations, laws, and oversight bodies that ensure data privacy and security, as well as private-sector initiatives, such as many social media companies' recent attempts to reduce the spread of misinformation, or firms that institute encryption protocols and cybersecurity best practices.

Second, we explored *user experience*. This refers to the extent to which various sources of friction keep users from getting value out of their digital experiences. We documented two types of friction: First, there is what we refer to as "productive friction"—elements such as passwords, two-factor authentication, security questions, privacy notices, or even those annoying "select all the pictures with traffic lights" quizzes. These experiences may be frustrating, but they support security and privacy. Then there's "unproductive friction"—obstacles to using digital systems that don't offer any security benefit. These include shortcomings in digital infrastructure (for example, spotty cellular data coverage), limits in access (for example, high prices for internet access), and poor design (are e-commerce sites and online transaction tools seamless and reliable?).

Third, we looked at *user attitudes*, or how people felt about their digital ecosystems. How much do users in a given economy trust their government and business leaders to use their data responsibly and securely? To answer these questions, we examined data from surveys covering privacy concerns, fears about new technology, trust in scientific and governmental institutions, and more. Importantly, user attitudes don't necessarily correlate to their digital infrastructure's actual level of security—or to users' actual behavior. For example, in recent years, there has been growing skepticism about the accuracy of information spread on social media, and yet many users continue to rely on these platforms for news.

Finally, we explored *digital user behavior* to examine the extent to which people actually engage with their digital environment. If there are frictions in the digital ecosystem, are users willing to tolerate those frictions and use the tools anyway? If levels of trust are low, does that lack of trust actually keep people from engaging with digital systems? To explore these questions, we looked at a variety of data, including consumer trends, social media usage, the proliferation of e-commerce and mobile payments, and media consumption patterns.

Ultimately, the most important indicator of user trust is user action. Assuming similar experiences with similar levels of friction and a similar array of available alternatives, the more users actually complete a given transaction, the more we can infer that they trust the system enough to engage with it. For example, if two countries offer similar e-commerce environments, but a larger proportion of users in one country actually use those systems than in another, that indicates that the first country exhibits greater levels of behavioral trust.

Of course, these are all holistic metrics that depend on numerous factors. While a fully objective, apples-to-apples comparison would be impossible, we were able to map out these different components of digital trust across the world through an extensive analysis of almost 200 indicators from public and proprietary databases (including anonymized data from our partners Mastercard, Blue Triangle, GlobalWebIndex, and Akamai), ultimately enabling us to score 42 different global economies in each of these four dimensions (see table 13-1).

What Does It Take to Build Digital Trust?

Clearly, trust is not a constant as we circumnavigate the world. Our findings offer several insights for any organization looking to build digital trust:

TABLE 13-1

Digital trust around the world

Researchers scored the performance of 42 global economies in four key metrics on a 0-to-100 scale (higher scores correspond to higher levels of trust). The top 10 scores for each category are highlighted.

	Attitudes	Behavior	Environment	Experience
	How users feel about the digital trust environment	How engaged users are in the digital environment	The mechanisms to build trust in the digital environment	How users experience the digital trust environment
Argentina	49	47	33	31
Australia	40	51	59	55
Austria	57	34	67	51
Belgium	53	31	65	65
Brazil	29	65	30	29
Canada	47	52	62	57
China	61	100	18	64
Colombia	18	51	38	26
Denmark	69	46	73	62
Egypt	45	42	16	27

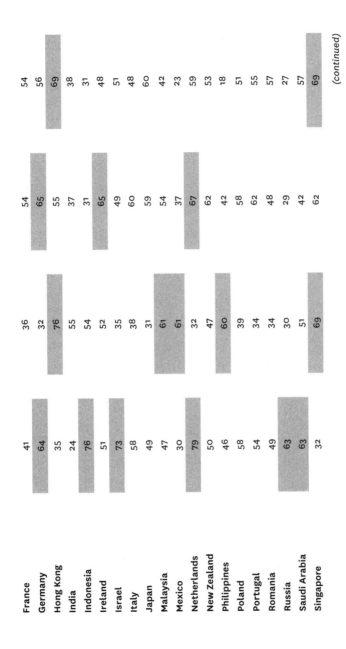

France	41	36	54	54
Germany	64	32	65	56
Hong Kong	35	76	55	69
India	24	55	37	38
Indonesia	76	54	31	31
Ireland	51	52	65	48
Israel	73	35	49	51
Italy	58	38	60	48
Japan	49	31	59	60
Malaysia	47	61	54	42
Mexico	30	61	37	23
Netherlands	79	32	67	59
New Zealand	50	47	62	53
Philippines	46	60	42	18
Poland	58	39	58	51
Portugal	54	34	62	55
Romania	49	34	48	57
Russia	63	30	29	27
Saudi Arabia	63	51	42	57
Singapore	32	69	62	69

(continued)

TABLE 13-1 (continued)

	Attitudes	Behavior	Environment	Experience
	How users feel about the digital trust environment	How engaged users are in the digital environment	The mechanisms to build trust in the digital environment	How users experience the digital trust environment
South Africa	38	41	41	30
South Korea	47	59	42	64
Spain	44	44	58	51
Sweden	77	59	68	60
Switzerland	63	27	68	68
Taiwan	33	66	53	62
Thailand	46	64	34	48
Turkey	33	53	30	35
United Arab Emirates	50	58	52	74
United Kingdom	47	56	65	55
United States	33	72	58	78
Vietnam	76	53	31	43

Source: Bhaskar Chakravorti et al., "The Digital Intelligence Index," Digital Planet, The Fletcher School at Tufts University, December 2020.

1. Digital trust is not monolithic

The first main takeaway from this analysis is that a high score in one trust metric by no means guarantees a high score in another: Netherlands ranks first in attitudes and Switzerland ranks second in environment, while both score low in behavior; similarly, China is first in behavior but scored much lower in environment. Why is this? There are a few effects at play here.

First, as economies develop a more trustworthy digital environment, it's likely that users' standards also rise, and this is reflected in less-engaged behavior. For example, Switzerland's high environment score and low behavior score suggest that Swiss users may be accustomed to highly secure digital experiences, making them less tolerant of security issues and thus less open to trying new digital tools than users in less-developed economies.

In addition, attitudes and behaviors don't always line up. For instance, our data shows that the Dutch are very positive in their attitudes toward their digital systems, and yet their lower tolerance for friction in digital experiences means that their behavior doesn't reflect that trust. Similarly, in China, despite an environment that is seemingly much less conducive to trust, users remain highly engaged.

And of course, there are always differences that are simply due to specific cultural contexts. For example, our analysis suggests that both American and Brazilian users are fairly skeptical about their digital systems' trustworthiness, despite the fact that the United States in fact has a much more secure digital environment.

2. A trusted environment is likely highly digitally evolved and stable

To explore how trust correlated with various metrics of digital growth, we compared the Digital Trust Scorecard with our Digital Evolution Scorecard, which categorized economies based on their level of digital evolution and current pace of digital growth.[2] We found that a secure digital environment and highly trusting attitudes were associated with digital evolution and stability, as exemplified by countries such as Denmark, Germany, Austria, and Sweden.

On the other hand, economies with high digital momentum tended to have less-secure digital environments, and their users often had greater privacy concerns. This means that as economies ramp up their digital momentum, it is especially important for government and business leaders to address privacy and security issues that may impact users.

3. Both mature, stable economies and less-developed, rapidly growing economies engender trust

Mapping digital trust attitudes onto our Digital Evolution Scorecard also revealed another interesting pattern: High-evolution, low-momentum economies and low-evolution, high-momentum economies both tended to have more positive attitudes toward their digital systems than economies that scored similarly on evolution and momentum.

For example, high-evolution, low-momentum economies such as those of many EU countries have been at the forefront of digital inclusion and data privacy regulations, which can engender greater trust in the digital ecosystem. Conversely, low-evolution, high-momentum economies such as those of Vietnam and Indonesia have been enthusiastic in adopting new technologies, leading many users to feel excited and open-minded toward these tools (despite a less-robust digital environment). But countries with low evolution and low momentum, as well as countries with high evolution and high momentum, both exhibited similarly low levels of trust, suggesting it may be helpful for these economies to work on building more positive attitudes toward digital infrastructure.

4. The combination of high digital evolution and high momentum engenders engaged users

While some less digitally evolved but high-momentum economies (for example, China, Indonesia, India, and Vietnam) exhibited highly engaged user behavior, in general, economies that combine high levels of digital evolution and digital momentum have the most highly engaged users (for example, Singapore, Hong Kong, and South Korea). That's in large part because these highly evolved yet still rapidly growing economies tend to offer seamless, smooth user experiences, while their consumers still tend to have a healthy appetite for trying new technologies—making them more tolerant of frictions and thus more likely to engage in digital experiences.

. . .

Importantly, while a lot of focus tends to be directed toward the role of guarantors of trust—that is, the governments and institutions that build and regulate our digital ecosystems—users themselves also have a major role to play in fostering trust in our collective digital ecosystem. In the digital world, it's not just companies that create the industry, and it's not just regulators who determine its security. The vast majority of digital content is user-generated, and much of security and data privacy comes down to how individual users engage with these systems.

There have been many calls recently for increased data and content regulation, but it's equally essential that policy makers and technologists invest in building awareness of cyber risks and misinformation among users. This can take the form of professional workshops, data literacy courses, or even media education classes geared toward fostering good habits early on.

But most importantly, any economy's trust-building interventions—at both the institutional and individual levels—must be proactive, forward-looking, and fine-tuned to the unique behaviors, attitudes, experiences, and environment of its digital ecosystem. But trust is not static concept: It varies depending on your perspective, priorities, and local context. Understanding the geography of digital trust will be essential to rebuilding it—and to sustaining trust in the rebuilding process itself.

Widely admired former Secretary of State George Shultz once said, "When trust was not in the room, good things did not happen. Everything else is details." As we envision a new normal for our global digital ecosystem, we cannot allow distrust to cast its shadow over the tools and technologies that bind us all together. To ensure that trust stays in the room, we must endeavor instead to foster a digital environment that prioritizes—and is worthy of—the trust of its users.

TAKEAWAYS

A study of digital trust in 42 countries examined four components: the security of an economy's digital environment; the quality of the digital user experience; the extent to which users report trust in their digital environment; and the extent to which users actually use the digital tools available to them. Their discoveries include:

✓ Digital trust is not monolithic. A high score in one trust metric by no means guarantees a high score in another.

✓ A trusted environment is likely stable and highly digitally evolved. On the other hand, economies with high digital momentum tend to have less-secure digital environments, and their users often have greater privacy concerns.

✓ Both mature, stable economies and less-developed, rapidly growing economies engender trust.

NOTES

1. Digital Planet, "Digital in the Time of COVID," https://sites.tufts.edu/digitalplanet/digitalintelligence/.

2. Bhaskar Chakravorti, Ajay Bhalla, and Ravi Shankar Chaturvedi, "Which Economies Showed the Most Digital Progress in 2020?," hbr.org, December 18, 2020, https://hbr.org/2020/12/which-economies-showed-the-most-digital-progress-in-2020.

Adapted from content posted on hbr.org, February 25, 2021 (product #H06765).

About the Contributors

RUSHDA AFZAL is a manager with Accenture Research and is based in Detroit.

BEENA AMMANATH is the executive director of the global Deloitte AI Institute and founder of the nonprofit Humans For AI, and also leads Trustworthy and Ethical Tech for Deloitte. She is an award-winning senior executive with extensive global experience in AI and digital transformation, spanning e-commerce, finance, marketing, telecom, retail, software products, services, and industrial domains with companies such as HPE, GE, Thomson Reuters, British Telecom, Bank of America, e*trade, and a number of Silicon Valley startups. She also serves on the advisory board at Cal Poly College of Engineering and has been a board member and adviser to several startups.

JANET BALIS leads EY's consulting professionals in the Americas focused on the customer agenda and revenue growth, including commercial excellence, customer experience, and product innovation and also leads EY's CMO practice. She has served as a partner at Betaworks, publisher of the *Huffington Post*, and executive vice president of media sales and marketing at Martha Stewart Living Omnimedia. Balis is on the global board of the Mobile Marketing Association and the International Television Academy of Arts and Sciences, and she is an adviser to the Harvard Business School Digital Initiative. Follow her on Twitter @digitalstrategy.

AJAY BHALLA is the president of Cyber & Intelligence (C&I) Solutions for Mastercard. He also sits on the company's management committee and is a senior fellow at the Fletcher School's Council on Emerging Market Enterprises.

CHRISTIAN CATALINI is the chief economist of the Diem Association and Diem Networks US, and cocreator of Diem (formerly Libra). He is also the founder of the MIT Cryptoeconomics Lab and a research scientist at MIT.

BHASKAR CHAKRAVORTI is the dean of global business at the Fletcher School at Tufts University and founding executive director of Fletcher's Institute for Business in the Global Context. He is the author of *The Slow Pace of Fast Change*.

RAVI SHANKAR CHATURVEDI is the director of research, doctoral research fellow for innovation and change, and a lecturer in international business at Fletcher's Institute for Business in the Global Context at Tufts University.

JULIE COFFMAN is Bain & Company's chief diversity officer and global leader of the firm's Diversity, Equity & Inclusion practice.

JONATHAN FRICK is a partner with Bain & Company's Technology and Cloud Services practice.

KC GEORGE is a partner in Bain & Company's Operating Model and Results Acceleration practices.

BHASKAR GHOSH is Accenture's chief strategy officer and a member of the firm's global management committee. He is a coauthor of *The Automation Advantage*.

TIM GLOMB is vice president of content and data at Cheetah Digital and founder of Audience Sherpa. A 20-year brand marketer, his experience is rooted at the intersection of content and technology with senior roles in music, TV, and, most recently, enterprise technology.

STEVE KACZYNSKI is an avid NFT collector who provides NFT market commentary for the Decentralized Generation Network (dgen.network). His professional background is in communications, with a focus on public relations and marketing at large corporations.

SCOTT DUKE KOMINERS is the MBA Class of 1960 Associate Professor of Business Administration in the Entrepreneurial Management Unit at Harvard Business School and a faculty affiliate of the Harvard Department of Economics. Prior to that, he was a junior fellow at the Harvard Society of Fellows and the inaugural Saieh Family Fellow in Economics at the Becker Friedman Institute.

DAVE LIGHT is a director of Thought Leadership Development at Accenture Research and is based in Boston.

MICHAEL LUCA is the Lee J. Styslinger III Associate Professor of Business Administration at Harvard Business School and a coauthor (with Max H. Bazerman) of *The Power of Experiments.*

JOE LUI is the global robotics practice lead for Accenture and is based in Seattle.

JAI MASSARI is a partner in the Financial Institutions Group of Davis Polk & Wardwell LLP and is outside counsel to Diem.

FIONA SCOTT MORTON is the Theodore Nierenberg Professor of Economics at the Yale University School of Management. Her research area is the economics of competition with a focus on health-care markets and antitrust enforcement. She served as deputy assistant attorney general for economic analysis at the Antitrust Division of the Department of Justice under President Obama.

KARTHIK NARAIN leads Accenture's cloud business.

RAGHAV NARSALAY is global research lead on Industry X for Accenture and is based in Mumbai.

ANDREW NG is the founder and CEO of Landing AI, the former vice president and chief scientist of Baidu, co-chair and cofounder of Coursera, the former founding lead of Google Brain, and an adjunct professor at Stanford University.

MARK PURDY is an independent economics and technology adviser based in London.

JONATHON REILLY is cofounder of Akkio, a no-code AI platform.

IDA NAIR SHARMA is an associate manager with Accenture Research and is based in Gurgaon, India.

RAHUL TELANG is Trustee Professor of Information Systems at the Heinz College, Carnegie Mellon University. His research focus is information security and the digital-media industry.

Index

"Adam Bomb," 20
addiction bias, 134. *See also*
    biases
Alcott, Hunt, 139
Amazon Go, 44
Ariely, Dan, 132
artificial intelligence (AI), xii,
    xvi, 93–94
    AI-enabled "predictive
      touch" technology, 46
    AI-powered technology, 49,
      51, 53
    challenges facing AI adoption
      in non-tech industries, 94–96
    data-centric AI development,
      96–98, 101
    small companies experienc-
      ing benefits of, 104, 110
    transition to MLOps, 98–100,
      101
    voice-enabled, 48
automation of warehouse
    operations
    growth opportunities for
      workers, 122–123
    investment in safety, 124–125

sense of workers' perspectives
    about, 114–115
training for workers, 123–124
workers' concerns related to,
    115–121, 125

balance limits, 36
Battersea Dogs and Cats Home,
    51
biases
    addiction and present, 134
    behavioral, 130–131
    customer inattention, 131–132
    default, 133–134
    reference dependence and
      framing effects, 132–133
biometrics, 47–48, 53
Bitcoin, 28, 39
blockchain technology, 8, 15–16,
    38
    blockchain-based digital
      diplomas, 20
    public and private sectors
      role in, 31
    See also crypto technology

Bored Ape Yacht Club, 18
Braghieri, Luca, 139
Brainard, Lael, 27
brand marketing, 6, 7
    entrance planning, 8–9
    keeping balance, 9
    looking for applications, 8
    targeting audiences or cus-
        tomers, 7
    watching competition, 8

Carrefour partnering with
    Google Assistant, 49
cash, 30, 33
    digital, 36, 40
    physical, 36, 40
    transfer programs, 28
central bank digital currency
    (CBDC), 27, 29, 35–38, 40
central banks, 28, 30, 36
Cheetah Digital (enterprise
    marketing platform), 78
Choi, James, 134
cloud computing, xiii, 65–66
    cloud capabilities, 69–70
    data security in, 67–68, 73
    importance of, 66–67
    maintaining legacy systems,
        68–69, 73
    need for skill development,
        72–73, 74
    shifting work to cloud sys-
        tem, 70–71, 74

club membership in NFT
    projects, 21
community-based NFT projects,
    25
conditional cash transfer
    programs, 28
consumers, 7, 24, 75, 77
    with behavioral biases, 131
    information sharing, 78,
        131–132
    interest in personalized offers, 77
    internet companies, 93, 94, 95
    protection, 31, 130, 139
    public sector connection
        with, 31
    sentiment, xii
contactless commerce, 42–43
    biometric data use for, 48
    imperatives for success, 50–53
    pay by face or voice, 47–48
    seamless digital transac-
        tions, 43–45
    sensor technologies, 48–50, 53
    technological advancements,
        45–47
content creation, addictive,
    138–140
cookies, 75, 79, 80
    function of, 75–76
Covid-19 pandemic/lockdown,
    xi, 42
    impact in IT industries, 55
    use of remote networks and
        systems during, 85

crypto technology
  cryptocurrencies, 27, 28, 39
  crypto markets, 24
  drawback of, 23
  See also blockchain technology
customer(s)
  "dead zone" between home
    and store, 51, 54
  decision-making, 138
  engagement, 79
  exploitation, 129–130
  in-store experiences, 53
  inattention, 131–132
  use of contactless technology
    for, 50–51
  zero-party data used to con-
    trol, 78–79

Dapper Labs, 14, 17, 18, 23
data
  breach in Equifax, 83, 85
  collection, xiii–xiv, 77
  cookies' role in collecting, 75–76
  data-centric AI development,
    96–98, 101
  privacy, xiii
  science for small businesses,
    104–105
  security in cloud computing,
    67–68
  sharing, xiv
  third-party, 76–77
  zero-party, 76–79

Decentraland, 5, 7
decision-making, 130–131
decoy pricing, 133
default bias, 133–134. *See also*
    biases
DEI strategy. *See* diversity,
    equity, and inclusion strat-
    egy (DEI strategy)
deposit stablecoins, 34–35, 37,
    40
digital addiction, 134, 139
digital art market, 17
digital consumer protection,
    140–141
digital currencies, xii
  Bitcoin, 28, 39
  CBDC, 27, 29, 35–38, 40
  cryptocurrencies, 27, 28, 39
  Ethereum, 28, 39
  See also non-fungible tokens
    (NFTs)
digital design, 141
  addictive content creation,
    138–140
  customer exploitation and,
    129–130
  using default settings, 137
  easy cancellation of service,
    136–137
  framing choices, 138
  regulation leveling digital
    playing field, 140–141
  systematic behavioral biases,
    130, 131–134, 141

digital design (*continued*)
  transparency in prices and
    fees, 135–136
digital ecosystems
  trust in, 146, 155, 157–158
  user attitudes in, 147
digital environment, 146–147,
    153–155, 158
Digital Evolution Scorecard,
    154, 155
digitalization, 145–146
digital olfaction, 46
digital trust, 146, 156
  digital environment, 146–147
  digital evolution and stabil-
    ity, 154–155, 158–159
  digital user behavior, 148
  insights to build, 149
  non-monolithic nature of,
    153–154, 158
  trust-building interventions,
    157
  user action, 148–149
  user attitudes, 147–148
  user experience, 147
  variation in key components
    of, 146
  around the world, 150–152
Digital Trust Scorecard, 146,
    153–154
digital user behavior, 148
Dirty Lemon, 44
diversity, equity, and inclusion
  strategy (DEI strategy), 58–59

Eichmeyer, Sarah, 139
employees
  authorization for, 87, 89
  training about threat of
    phishing attacks, 86–87,
    89
  use of no-code tools for,
    105
  See also workers concerns
    related to automation
Equifax, data breach in, 83–84,
    85
Ericson, Keith, 138
Ethereum, 28, 39
Everydays: The First 5000 Days,
    13
externality, 84

Facebook, 79
FedEx, 123
Fortnite, 4–5
Foundation, 14

General Data Protection Regu-
    lation (GDPR), 76
Gensler, Gary, 27, 37
Gentzkow, Matt, 139
GitHub, 58
global warehouse automation
    market, 113–114
Google, 79, 132
Gutter Cat Gang, 18, 19

high-evolution, low-momentum economies, 155–156, 159
holographic technology, 49–50
HubSpot, 60
Hundreds, The (streetwear brand), 20

infrastructure as a service (IaaS), 69, 70, 73
in-house phishing simulations, 87
interoperability, xiii, 35, 39

JD.Com, 44
"Jenkins the Valet" project, 18
Jin, Ginger Zhe, 132
job loss, fear of, 115–116, 126
Just Walk Out technology, 44

Kaseysa, 84
koodos, 14, 20

Laibson, David, 134
legacy system maintenance for cloud computing, 68–69, 73
"lickable screen," 47
"lift-and-shift" strategy, 69
Light, Dave, 65
low-evolution, high-momentum economies, 155–156, 159
Luca, Michael, 132

machine learning operations (MLOps), 96, 98–101
Madrian, Brigitte, 134
Magic Mirror, 45
Martin, Daniel, 132
Massachusetts Health Connector, 138
Meta, 20
metaverses, xii, 3–4
  brand marketing in, 7–9
  business applications in, 5
  commercial applications of, 6
  environment of, 5
  social media landscape, 6–7
MetaVRse, 5
Metrick, Andrew, 134
Microsoft, 5
MLOps. See machine learning operations (MLOps)
Moderna, 65–66
Morton, Fiona M. Scott, 139

National Institutes of Health, 65
NBA Top Shot, 14, 17, 18, 23
Nifty Gateway, 14
Nike, 6
"no-code" platforms, 104, 110
  advantage of, 106
  AI platform, 105–106
  features, 107–108, 111
  finding right platform, 108–111
  for small businesses, 104–105

non-fungible tokens (NFTs),
xii, 7, 8, 13–14
ability to manage crypto
market swings, 24
ecosystems, 17–20
future of, 24–25
maintaining community
engagement, 22–23
need for on-ramps for new
users, 23–24
as tool for market design, 15–17
use of, 21
See also digital currencies
non-tech industries, challenges
facing AI adoption in, 94
cost of customization, 95–96
gap between proof of concept
and production, 96
small data sets, 95
Nvidia, 5

Office of the Comptroller of the
Currency (OCC), 33–34
OpenSea, 14
"opt-out" design, 137
ownership, 15
in NFT communities, 15,
19–21, 24, 25
of online image or animation, 14

PaaS. See platform as a service
(PaaS)

patch management, 87, 89
pay by face or voice, 47–48
phishing attacks, 86–87, 89
platform as a service (PaaS), 69,
70, 74
POAP, 20
Powell, Jerome, 27
Predictably Irrational (Ariely), 132
present bias, 134. See also biases
prevention of ransomware
attacks, 86
data back up, 88, 89
priority to patch vulnerabilities, 87, 89
training to employees about
threat of phishing attacks,
86–87, 89
private sector, 29, 30, 36
incentives, 39
role in blockchain technology, 31
productive friction, 147
public sector
and CBDCs, 37
guidance, 39
involvement in stablecoins,
29–30
role in blockchain technology, 31

radio-frequency-identification
tags (RFID tags), 43–45, 53
ransomware attacks, 84–85
functionality of, 86, 88–89

prevention steps to secure
from, 86–88, 89
See also prevention of ransomware attacks
reference currency, 32–33
reference dependence and
framing effects, 132–133
regulators, 28, 30, 38, 76, 80, 84
renminbi, digital, 29, 32
retailers
benefit from monitoring of
stock flows, 44
creating content-rich experiences, 51
in-store experiences, 42, 53
introducing interactive fitting rooms, 45
use of contactless technology for, 50–51
RFID tags. *See* radio-frequency-
identification tags (RFID
tags)
Roblox, 5
Rosenquist, James Niels, 139
RTFKT, 6

SaaS. *See* software as a service
(SaaS)
"same risks, same rules"
approach, 31
seamless digital transactions,
43–45
sensor technologies, 48–50, 53

Sephora, 45
services, ease of cancellation,
136–137
Shultz, George, 157–158
skill development for cloud
computing, 72–73, 74
Slack, 59
social media, 6, 19, 77, 134,
139, 148
software as a service (SaaS), 69,
70, 73
Sotheby's, 7
stablecoins
benefits of, 28
CBDCs, 27, 29, 35–38, 40
deposit, 34–35, 37, 40
as form of private money, 30–31
regulation of, 38–39
risk of, 28–30
true, 32–34, 37–38, 40
See also digital currencies
Starc, Amanda, 138
store reinvention, 51–52
StubHub, 132, 135–136
SupDucks, 18, 19
sustainability, 8, 70, 71, 74
systematic behavioral biases, 131.
See also biases

Tastry, 49
Teams (Mesh platform), 5
technology-neutral regulation,
31

technology talent
    competition among compa-
        nies to recruit, 56–57
    demand for, 55–56, 60–61
    workplace environment factors
        for attracting, 58–61
third-party data, 76–77, 80
Touchless.ai, 48
TriMirror, 45
true stablecoins, 32–34, 37–38, 40

unconscious-bias training, 57
Uniqlo, 45
United States
    average cost of data breach in, 85
    employees in warehouse and
        storage sector in, 114
    Federal Trade Commission, 83
Unity, 5
unproductive friction, 147
U.S. Federal Trade Commission,
    130

VeVe application, 14
virtual agents, 49, 53
voice-enabled AI, 48
voice genomics, 47–48

Weinstein, Samuel, 139
"wildcat stablecoins," 31
Wilson, H. James, 65

workers concerns related to
    automation
    fear of job loss, 115–116, 126
    higher-quality work, 120–121
    inadequate training, 116–118,
        126
    increased speed and effi-
        ciency, 119–120
    optimistic about automation,
        119, 126
    safety, 119
    unreliable technology, 118
workforce environment
    factors
    accountable senior manage-
        ment, 59, 61
    culture of coaching and
        development, 59–60, 61
    diversity and inclusion,
        commitment to, 58–59, 61

Yale Tobin Center for Economic
    Policy report, 140
YouTube, 139

zero-party data, xii, 76–77
    data collection from custom-
        ers, 78–79
    future of customer engage-
        ment, 79
    personalization in, 77–78
Zhang, Jeffery, 37